T0157034

Grieving After the Death of a Child

a personal perspective

Denice Parks-Hayes

iUniverse, Inc.
Bloomington

Grieving After the Death of a Child
A Personal Perspective

iUniverse books may be ordered through booksellers or by contacting:
iUniverse
1663 Liberty Drive
Bloomington, IN 47403
www.iuniverse.com
1-800-Authors (1-800-288-4677)

ISBN: 978-1-4620-3620-2 (sc)
ISBN: 978-1-4620-3621-9 (e)

Printed in the United States of America

iUniverse rev. date: 8/26/2011

special dedication to:

*All the Victims of Gun Violence and the loved ones
they leave behind
To my Uncles, Aunts and cousins, who have lost their
battle of life. I love you all very much
and the memories of the time we have shared will
remain with me.

a special thanks to:

My Uncle's, Aunt's and Cousin's who showed special support and love during the time I lost Tarrence, I thank you and any others that may have played a special role in helping at such a devastating time, for loving me, supporting me and stepping up to assist out of love and not obligation, that's what a family does. I love you and thank you from the bottom of my heart:

Mrs. Angela M. Evans (Victor) My cousin with whom I've always shared a special bond, she was right at my side through every step of this horrible day. Thank you Victor for being patient and understanding.

My special friends and neighbors, who were so supportive during such a bad time in my life.

  (a) Mary Morris, Author of Young Lions: Who
      encouraged me to give birth to my vision
  (b) Phyllis Duncan Founder of MOMS Support
      Group "Mothers of Murdered sons":

MOMS allowed me the freedom to grieve without being judged, to express my feelings of grief and to cry endlessly. Thank you Ms. Duncan, for giving birth to a Support Group that has not only touched my life but also the lives of many other women and families whose lives have also been upset by street violence, and are in need of an outlet for their grief. Including yourself, who also lost your son to street violence in May, 2005.

* And most of all I thank GOD for planting the seed called Tarrence Darnell Parks Sr. also nicknamed Bookie. For without God he would have never come to exist. Thank you God for the time you loaned Tarrence to me.

A Mother's love is forever!
My Pain
My pain has a name, it's called longing
I long for what was and what might have been
And what will no longer be.
Author: Unknown

Grief will turn to joy
You will weep and mourn while the world rejoices.
You will grieve, but your grief

will turn to joy. A woman giving birth to a child has
pain because her time has come,

but when her baby is born She forgets the anguish
because of her joy that a child is born

into the world. So with you, now is your time of grief,
But I will see you again and you will rejoice, and no
one will take away your joy.

John 16: 20-22

book reviews

This Autobiography is emotionally capturing! It depicts a Mothers most inner pain and suffering due to and after the loss of an only child (A Son). I think this Author laid out the endless endurance of grieving. I sincerely hope that this book will be an inspiration, an example, a lesson and perhaps a solution for choices made especially by Young Men, because Parents and Guardians experience extreme and un-controllable worries for their Children and their Loved ones!.

Congratulations, Denice

" THUMBS UP! "

----Jannie Earl-----

This book will help others because some people don't know how to let go of things and let their feelings out without being ashamed.

Losing a loved one changes your whole life and the lives of those around you also. Healing comes with time, but having family around helps a great deal too.

I didn't know the depth of Denice's hurt and pain until actually reading the book and my heart hurts for her. This book is so full of emotion that you can feel both the pain and emotion. I hurt too while reading this book, it brought tears to my eyes.

Reading this book gives a realistic view of the hurt Denice Hayes felt to lose not only her child, but her only child. I believe this book will help others because it actually talks about the grief process. Denice talked about the levels of pain she went through as she grieved her loss. It will help others understand the grief process and what to expect as they go through it and how important it is to be strong and seek counseling.

Florece McDaniels

contents

foreword

Your book is a book on grieving, healing and hope.
And those who review your book will comment on
how
"Grieving after the Death of a Child" has encouraged
them to
grieve, heal, forgive, and to go on with life.
Many women don't know it yet but they need to read
your book so that they too may begin their healing
process.
Mary Morris
Author: Young Lions

preface
death vs. murder

Are there different levels of grief after losing a loved one?

I do believe that there are different levels of grief, and I also believe that death is the most traumatic experience any person could endure, especially the death of a child. It has been often said that death may be more mentally acceptable, if a person has been sick before death, rather than a sudden or traumatic death such as murder or an accident.

The death of the person with a history of being **sick** or previously sick will have allowed the family a period of time to slowly accept or digest the fact that the person will/may parish. This is different than that of the family who loses a loved one to a **traumatic or sudden death,** such as murder or a car accident. A sudden death deprives you of time to mentally prepare mentally or to digest and accept the death, it comes as a shock. The loss hurt tremendously.

Both loved one are gone, it's just the matter that one has allowed the family time to mentally accept death and the other is **forced** to deal with the loss. I think that each circumstance has its own grieving period. I lost my father to emphysema, my maternal grandmother to kidney failure related to diabetes and my grandfather to prostate cancer. I also lost three cousin's two to sickness and one to a car accident, and it hurt deeply. These are periods in my life that I will also never forget.

We grieve the loss of our loved ones only differently, depending upon the circumstances of the death, and who it is that you have lost. Don't get me wrong we love or should love all of our loved ones and are hurt when we lose them; I believe that the grief process may vary.

Reviewing the various instances of death I believe that each instance of loss is most assuredly accompanied by a great sense of loss and sadness linked to the grieving process/period. For example; a death that was instant such as a car accident, murder, and sudden sickness long/short term (prior knowledge).

The different instances of death are:

- ◆ Death after sickness
- ◆ Death by vehicular accident
- ◆ Death by murder
- ◆ Death of one of your children
- ◆ Death of an only child
- ◆ Death of a child by a another sibling

- ♦ Sickness (Prior or no knowledge and mental preparedness)
- ♦ Loss of one child vs. only child
- ♦ Vehicle accident (instant vs. prolonged)
- ♦ Murder (solve vs. unsolved).

Families that lose a loved one to a long term sickness has been allowed some mental preparedness, while they will and do grieve I believe that there may be more acceptance of the loss because they knew what the outcome would be, it does however, mean that they are any more willing to release that loved one upon death.

Murder (unsolved vs. solved)

I believe that these families grief takes place on a different level. Depression may play a part in it because unlike other deaths these deaths are different in the sense that more issues are involved.

Unsolved murder - These families lose their child or loved one, yet the murder is unsolved and may go through or experience the anguish of additional pain/ suffering due to the fact that those responsible for the death of their loved one has not been brought to justice, remaining free, not held accountable for their actions and they have to accept that this person may never be found or brought to Justice also leaving unresolved questions, and this family may often harbor a sense of injustice on behalf of the loss of their loved one due to their circumstance,

Solved murders – This family may experience all of the same symptoms except with closure when the murderer has been brought to justice. Ultimately there is some closure for the family's loss for a death related to a solved murder vs. that of an unsolved murder.

♦ Death of an only child

I believe that families do grieve, however the experience of losing an only child, I believe the level of grief differs because it's an **only child** lost and they carry the additional burden that he/she is all I had, no one left at home. My only child dead/murdered and possibly unsolved therefore no one held accountable this loss also goes to another level of grief because in many ways I believe it often forces "empty nest syndrome" which is often spoken of when the child(ren) finish school or move out.

Other thoughts a family may carry are things such as I will never see my child marry, have children, be a grandmother and so these thoughts are thoughts that may take the grief to another level, also possibly further the depression in some, extending the grieving process thus hindering the introduction back into society, or day to day reality.

Another obstacle of the inability to bounce back or cause excessive emotional depression after the murder of a child is if you have other boys and live in certain environments that may not be positive. Drugs/Gangs, may increase the inability to move pass the grieving process because of the fear of suffering a similar loss again, this may cause the inability to focus on moving pass the grieving process which again takes you to yet another level of grief.

I think that psychological counseling or even temporary medication may be necessary and definitely suggested due to the fact that the grieving process is mentally draining and not everyone may be strong enough to handle the process on their own.

I asked various individuals who had experienced the death of a loved from sickness or had experienced the murder of a loved one, what their thoughts were related to the difference in the grieving process and this is what some of them had to say:

Florece Mc Daniels - Had a daughter to die of pneumonia and grandson to be murdered and she stated though all death she feels is traumatic, however death by murder is by far the most emotional and painful, leaving a void and emptiness and the shock of something so traumatic is overwhelming to accept.

Judy Thomas – Has never lost a child but she has experienced the murder of her younger brother and in November 2005 she experienced the sudden death of her Mother due to sudden illness, with whom she was very close. And she stated that since she had not lost a child she couldn't speak to that, but she has said that if the pain is anything compared to the devastation of losing her mom then she could not imagine it because of the hurt and pain she has endured and continues to deal with daily. She admits that it is still a struggle especially during the Holidays; she becomes emotional sadness still lives within.

Gladys Robinson – Has experienced three sudden deaths: (1) A Sister who was murdered, (2) A Brother who died suddenly of a heart attack and her (3) Mother who died of an asthma attack. Mrs. Robinson states that the grief was different for her in each instance.

She states that while it was very difficult losing each of her loved ones, losing her mother was the most devastating and emotionally intense for her. She credits her relationship with God as her source for getting through this difficult time, and she agrees indeed that grief for her did indeed have different levels because she has experienced them herself.

Darnell Person – Stated that death by sickness in his opinion was an act of God. Death by murder however is a criminal act and the loved one is taken, therefore this impacts the grieving process, causing it to be more emotional.

Jesses Hayes – Experienced an unexpected death due to sickness of the grandmother that raised me and I thought losing my Grandmother was hard, it didn't compare to the loss of my Step-Son. While my son is alive, Tarrence was like a son to me also because I raised him from the age of five and you don't expect to bury your child. Your child is your life and to lose a child your life almost stops, in a sense your life dies or very close to it.

acknowledgments:

Jesse Hayes - My wonderful husband, thank you for your love, friendship, patience and most of all your total support in everything, you have been at my side and I love you, though I know you also grieve in your own way you were always there for me.

Florece Mc Daniels - My Mother, I thank God for you and I will always cherish the special relationship that we share, you are not only my mom but my friend and confidant, always there for me, and I Love you dearly.

Tarrence Darnell Parks Jr. - My only grandchild I love you and I know that you will miss your dad and I know your Dad loved you very much. I am very proud of you and will always be there for you. "Be all that you can be and do it well."

My oldest son (by marriage) - Eric A. Hayes, his wife, LaToya and the two youngest grandsons. Eric Jr. and Bryce, I love you all and I am very proud of you.

My Sister - Willestine Parks - Thank you for the strength that you had when I couldn't find mine, for your continuous support, friendship and being "THE BEST" Sister a girl could have.

My Brother - James W. Nelson II, I want you to know that I love you very much and I am glad you are my brother, thank you for being there for Tarrence. You are also a wonderful example of a loving father.

My Nieces and Nephews - Taneesha (Jason), James III, Janee, Briana, Joshua, life is short live it to the fullest, be happy, be safe, make good choices, continue to love and cherish life and each other and stay close I love you all.

My extended family – Derotha Burns my (Mother in-law) and Family. Thank you for being there at such a painful time in my life and for loving Tarrence as you did, I love you all.

My Step-Father – James W. Nelson Sr., his wife, Verna, I thank you for being a wonderful parent as I grew up. I love you for all that you taught me growing up, the love, support, the time you gave as a father and the discipline that helped me to be who I am today.

Tarrence's biological Father - Darnell Person I know that you had your own special bond and I know that he loved you. Tarrence is gone but that is a time in our lives we will forever share, May God bless you and your family.

My Father Preston Webb (Decease) Tarrence Sr's Maternal Grand dad and my step-mom Onetha

My Grandparents - Samuel and Earnestine Parks: My Daddy Boe and Muh' Dear (both deceased.)

Tarrence Sr's Paternal Grand Parents - Samuel Hopkins and Mattie L. Person, (both deceased.)

Peggy Ann Kelly – The Mother of My Grandson (Tarrence Darnell Parks Jr.)

Thank you for loving my son, enough to give him a son and for loving them both enough to bring my grandson into this world.

The following letter I found written by a parent who had lost two children and I would like to share it with parents who have lost children in death but especially to murder:

A Letter to Hurting Parents Who Have Lost Children

From a Parent Who Himself Has Lost Two Children.

I know the emptiness and pain you feel. It is beyond description. The closest I can say is that it is like someone cut your heart out, and along with it all your hope and dashed it on the floor before your eyes. Despite your wishes and prayers, this terrible thing will not just go away. Now you must face the unrelenting fact of that lifeless little one.

Though sin seems to triumph and wrong conquers right, though lies can put justice to flight, but God's truth is eternal. His word shows his might, and he will bring justice to light.
– Gustafson

The search for justice can be satisfied only by trusting the God who is always just.

B. Crowder

introduction
our last night together

November 2005: "Thanksgiving day" our family gathered for the holiday, at my house it was so strange this time because Tarrence who was always the last to show, would often miss some of the family. This particular time as my mom, sister and her girls prepared to leave Tarrence arrived. Tarrence Jr's, Mother who had not spent time with the family in a while came with my mom this holiday. They shared additional time together dialoguing and laughing. Tarrence teased his son's mom and before departing they hugged and kissed, as always when parting.

As I prepared Tarrence's dinner plate that fateful Thanksgiving evening, our older son and his family arrived after initially thinking they may not make it due to other obligations. After dinner I thought to myself, this is a perfect time to take a family picture since everyone is here together, which had never happened before.

I proceeded to try to figure out a way to take the picture, when the doorbell rang, it was my son's best friend. I asked him to take the picture. After taking our picture, I then took one of them together. In the past few months my son had begun to spend more time with his son, Tarrence Jr., who was playing junior basketball. Tarrence had not had the opportunity to watch games that had been videoed of Tarrence Jr's games. Together they watched Tarrence Jr's first trip to Disney World, they played several games of air hockey together. That night as I think about it they seemed to be bonding and catching up on time they had lost together.

As always, I videoed taped the evening. As the night winded down, I remember the B.E.T. Awards were on and Alicia Keys sang her then new song "Unbreakable." As the 10 o'clock hour approached my son prepared to leave with his friend. We hugged and Tarrence Jr. said dada don't forget my basketball game on Saturday, saying this will be my last two games.

That night would be the last night my son would share with us, the last night we had the opportunity to lay our eyes on him, the last meal he would share with his family. As he left he left his love offerings of hugs, kisses, and a special handshake with my husband. Oddly, my husband remembers he did the handshake twice that night. As they left I watched my son walk away, slow and gracefully. I had no idea that it would be the last time I would see my son alive, a day never to be forgotten, because it is the day that truly changed our lives FOREVER.

chapter one
pronounced dead of a gunshot wound

I took the call at my mom's house on Friday, November 25, 2005: Around 5:00 in the evening, Tarrence has been shot. Hurry Tarrence's friend said, "His voice full of fear and urgency," he is being taken to a hospital on the West Side of Chicago. It was a weird thing, because I had imagined so many times this dreaded phone call might come if ever in the wee hours of the night that call when the phone rings at 2 or 3:00 a.m. with bad news. And oddly enough it turned out to be a call on Friday at dinner time. I called my sister to inform her of what had happened. And she and her girls met us at the hospital, as well as my brother in-law.

On the way to the hospital I can't describe the sensation that came over my body at that very moment; it is as though I went numb and blank all at the same time in disbelief, as though my mind and body had disassociated

1

with each other. All the way to the hospital it was as though I wasn't in my right thoughts it was as though I was outside of myself. I guess I was in a state of shock and disbelief.

We arrived at the hospital, pulling into the parking lot, my mine racing faster than it ever had and my heart was beating so fast with fear that it seemed as though I could hear it right in my ears. As we waited I tried not to think because I didn't want anything negative to enter my mind. We waited a while and a Chicago Policeman came in to ask questions about my son, another later asked questions about why he may have been in the area.

I sat there in this empty Emergency room looking around and thinking to myself, I can't believe I am here, this can't be real, seeming like a terrible nightmare, and all I wanted to do was to wake up. Sadly, it was not a nightmare and this street violence had come into my home and wrecked our lives!

Not long after the questions a male nurse from the emergency room came out to give us an update, it was now about 6:20 p.m. and the emergency room nurse told us that Tarrence wasn't doing very well. He had lost a lot of blood and was very sick. My husband then asked where Tarrence had been shot. The reply was one I was not prepared to hear. At that moment I felt my stomach drop to my feet, as an elevator does when it races to its crashing point and is about to crash. The male nurse's replied, "In the head."

Having worked in a hospital for eighteen years, I knew

when he said the head, closing my eyes I let out a sigh grabbing my mouth, as though saying oh my God! No, instantly realizing that this meant his chances were not good, and that it would be by the grace of God if he made it.

It was as though I had frozen up, my mind had stopped, I couldn't think, I was trying to catch up with all that was happening and it was all moving way too fast for me to grasp it. This was the longest night of my life. It was definitely the worst weekend and I won't ever forget. I remember having this sick feeling in my stomach and having to go to the bathroom several times, my stomach was a ball of nerves. That night was truly like an out of body experience. I kept feeling as though I was in a bad nightmare and was waiting any moment to wake up, feeling as though I was in a daze. Finally, after around 9:00 that evening and having moved us twice we were now in the waiting room for ICU and they were preparing to bring my son up, after working on him most of that evening which had been about four hours.

By then the hall and the waiting room was full of people family and friends of his and mine that had heard the horrible news rushing to the hospital to verify its truth. I didn't know how the news spread but there were many waiting for news on how he was doing and to see him.

Finally, they were allowing us to briefly visit, allowing immediate family in first. My husband and I went in first, and oh my God, I was not prepared to see my child laying there in such a state. A machine moving up and down breathing for him, tubes everywhere, his head bandaged, face wrapped, blood backing up out of his mouth as though it was water; this did not look like my child laying here that I had just seen alive and well the day before.

I stood there in this small hospital room in disbelief, still in a disassociated state, my world turned upside down, my heart was crushed, but somehow I held it together, I know that it was by the grace of God. It was that Peace that I had heard my Pastor speak of so often, "that peace of God" that surpasses all understanding I know that is what I was experiencing.

I stood to the side feeling as though this was an out of body experience my body was there yet my mind had still not accepted the reality of what was happening and was elsewhere. While standing outside the ICU room a young man walked up to me introduced himself and handed me a piece of paper, he said Ms. Parks I am so sorry for your loss and if there is anything, I mean anything! That I can do please don't hesitate to call me. I thanked him and put the small piece of paper away. To this day I don't remember his name or what happened to that piece of paper but I would like to say thank you to that person for the generosity he showed that day.

As family and friends went in to see Tarrence to verify the news they had heard many left out in disbelief, with tears rolling down their cheeks. Many young men as well as women, so distraught with grief sat with their face in their hands broken down in tearful states, some standing along walls crying, others leaving with tears streaming down their cheeks and I still couldn't believe this terrible thing was happening, It was unbelievable that this was actually happening but it was real, and I was associated with it, something I had often seen but hoped never to experience., the death of my child and in such a way no mother would ever think. Shot in the head by a stranger, left to die in the streets.

For some time I watched as my son's body reacted to the tubes inserted, especially the one in his mouth used to absorb the blood that was flowing continuously out of his mouth. His face swollen, I could see a short gash on his forehead between his eyes, maybe from where he had fallen. He didn't really look like himself but I knew it was my child, because a mother knows, and the tattoos I knew about were also confirmation that this was the child I had given birth to, my only child laying so near death by the hands of another human being.

As the long night went on, I noticed his fingers on the right hand, which I had held onto most of the night begin to stiffen, which I know was an indication to me that my baby was no more, that God had taken him, the body that lay there was empty of spirit and the machine was only blowing air into a lifeless body, yet I couldn't help holding onto a prayer and hope for a miracle that he would open his eyes or give some form of hope that he was still with us but it didn't happen.

The hospital continued to run test to confirm his state, and early that Saturday morning a staff person came in to share with the family that they had confirmed by tests that indeed the bullet that he had taken had damaged his brain beyond repair, beyond hope, saying that if he survived he would never be able to communicate, because of his severe condition and damage to his brain the bullet had caused. My child never opened his eyes!

I prayed that he knew we were right there at his side every moment and that he was never alone. Tarrence was full of life, promise, and adventure. He had a beautiful warm bright smile, a dimple in his chin and one in his left jaw and a huge heart. He loved to have fun.

My In-laws were also very supportive during this time; Tarrence had often spent lots of time at their home. We all stayed at the hospital until the very end as well as Tarrence's Dad, and many other friends and family members.

At about the 1:30 hour my sister and the oldest niece returned to the hospital, along with my mom who had not been at the hospital this entire time because she'd said that she didn't want to see Tarrence lying there, so my niece had kept her updated on his condition to this point.

Ma finally went in to spend time with her first and oldest grandson, who now lay in grave condition, after about twenty minutes she exited the room, tears running down her cheeks and sadness in her face, saying very little she went home.

Jesse and I left also to freshen up, once outside I returned a call to my grandson's mom who had been calling me repeatedly but I couldn't get a signal in the hospital to answer the call. Once connected the only thing she asked me was "Is it true?" And I said yes it is, after that all I heard was screaming in the background and the phone suddenly disconnected. I guess she'd heard about the shooting but needed to confirm it with me.

Gladys Robinson, a good neighbor had also called opening the door she was returning home also and stopped over, she stated that she had been concerned because she knew it wasn't like us to not let her know we weren't going to be home overnight. I then told her what had happened, she offered her condolesence and a hug and at that moment I sobbed profusely because I hurt so.

Gladys promised to keep a check on us and she did daily, also cooking for us many times. I appreciate the many other neighbors, who stopped over also, but Gladys was a constant and for that I thank her for all she did for us.

By now we had taken Tarrence Jr. to his mom while we took care of the many things that needed to be done. After leaving the hospital that night we went by my mom's to check on her because I knew she was quite upset when she left the hospital earlier that day.

As we pulled up I got a rush, my heart began beating fast and my mind went into replay of the day we got the call about Tarrence. As we walked into the house she was crying still so I hugged her, we talked and she spoke about how hurt she was over Tarrence being shot and that she never imagined something like this. She said that her heart was broken into a million pieces. I began to cry because I understood her pain and I too felt that my heart had shattered this day. A day we will not forget as long as we live.

Saturday, November 26, 2005: At 11:58 a.m. my son, Tarrence Darnell Parks at the age of twenty-eight years old was pronounced dead from a gunshot wound sustained on the streets of the West Side of Chicago in an area known as The Square.

chapter two
preparing to say good-bye

a s I sat at my computer preparing information for my son's Funeral, I remember thinking to myself how a person that didn't truly know him could take Tarrence's life, because he wasn't a bad person, he was full of love, he was a young man yes, who had made some bad choices as we all have, overall he was a kind, respectable, pleasant, and a very unselfish person, and most of all a human being that did not deserve to be murdered in the streets for any reason.

He had a very serious demeanor who also liked to have fun and had the promise of a future as a Sketch Artist or Barber. Tarrence cut hair on the side when he wasn't working of relatives and friends, he was such a talent for cutting hair that he could cut and add designs to even his own head when he cut it. Yes, he had a dream and someone robbed him of his dream and took his life from him – and I may never truly know who or why.

As I documented information that would be used for Tarrence's Funeral Services there were family members at my side, taking roles on the program such as Reading the Obituary, saying a prayer writing poems, and his Cousin even sang. We buried Tarrence in December 2005. It was a long walk to the front of the Church and an even longer service, as I sat staring at my son lying there. My body was there but my mind was off in another place, void and blank. I felt the tears as the rolled down my face.

At one point during the service I remember hearing my Sister-in-law yell out Tarrence's name as she cried, I watched as an old girlfriend leaned over into the casket as if still in disbelief. During the reviewal his current girlfriend stood in belief cradling herself, just standing there shaking. I finally went to her and lead her back to where we were sitting.

As my Pastor had said so often, a parent never imagines outliving their child(ren) rather just the opposite.

"Bearing people's burdens, shouldering their pain and grief,
Shows the love of Christ for others, bringing them his sure relief."

Author: Unknown

December 13, 2005: The funeral is over, and things begin to go back to normal for I have to go back to the real world of "work." Therefore I am left alone now, to deal with all that has transpired in my life over this two-week period so quickly, having had so many people to lean on and step in and handle many things to keep me from having to deal with it, and now I am face to face with the reality of all that has happened. Too much time on my hands because I am not working right now, and all I do is think about so many things, all day long my mind is just at it, it won't quit.

February 21, 2006: I tell you the murder of my son has put me in a state of shock, a disassociation with the world and everything in it for some time, because I was not prepared for my son's demise especially the way he was killed. I find myself in Disbelief, later withdrawal, choosing who I wanted to associate with or be around. I mourned more as I began to transition from the shock to the realization that my son is dead, and the person(s) responsible may never be prosecuted for their role in his murder seemed to make me even sadder and the idea more painful.

I had been told on several occasions that sadness could be seen in my face and eyes. People that had no idea that I was grieving and others that knew of my loss could see that I was still wrestling with the hurt and pain of losing my only child. Sometimes they would ask me how are you doing or are you okay? And just hearing them ask me those words knowing how I was hurting on the inside all I could do was cry, I couldn't hold them back and so the tears would come rushing out like the flood gates of a hurricane and I couldn't help it.

I now know the meaning of "my Joy is gone." This was the only way to describe that emptiness that now dwelled where I know that a heart is but that joy seemed to now be buried so deep down inside these days. I began to live my days as close to normal as I could, going through the motions of housework, paying bills etc. When the family would get together we would try hard to celebrate as much as we could but the funny thing about the mind and the body is sometimes they are not both in the same place and this was often the situation with me, the body was there but the mind was not.

Celebrating didn't seem as fulfilling as it once did and sometimes I cried on the inside while trying to smile on the outside, because of the sadness, and the many things that still dwelled in the back of my mind about my son.

By the grace of God I made it day by day. As the days got further I began to sleep a little, instead of walking the floor looking out of the window most of the night because I wasn't able to sleep because my mind wouldn't rest. As time moves forward I have found that there are a few days that seem close to normal, days when it doesn't hurt as much as it did to think about the fact that your child is gone, and the tears seem to be fewer and farther in between sometimes. But there are other times it seems as if it has just happened and the sadness, pain and tears come down on you like a hammer, almost to the point of being unbearable.

Overall, I have come to the conclusion that you never get over losing a child. I believe that the heart will always ache from the loss and the emptiness left behind and will never be the same again. It's almost like a black man when he gets that X on his back, he is labeled forever and the police never let him rest again forever harassing him. That's how the memories are, they are always with you. It's just that some days you handle them well and other days you don't.

November 15, 2006: I remember after my son's death, we stayed in contact with the police on a weekly basis in an effort to bring justice. We had hope in finding the person/s responsible for Tarrence's murder, it is almost one year later, the phone calls have slowed down and no contact has been made. It has gotten to a point where the detective barely returns the calls when we left messages.

It's really sad that the Police acted so unconcerned, and as though your loss is not a big deal to them, almost as if saying it's just another black man dead, and the hard thing about when someone is murdered is that it generally leaves such a strong desire for justice to be done and that is the only thing that will often help bring closure, I know for me I would like justice and closure for the murder of my only child as well as many others who have lost loved ones to murder.

Many days after my son's death, I had much time to myself because I had been laid off month's prior, and there I was with all of this time on my hands and no one to talk to because everyone is at work. My mind is racing miles a minute thinking about so many things. I had not been sleeping, still in somewhat of a daze and trying to digest all that has happened in this short quick timeframe.

I am now faced with accepting that my son is not coming back, that he is dead, yet somehow this still has not totally absorbed into my mind, it's still like a dream or a nightmare and I'm waiting to wake up. I would lie in bed at night for hours and hours at a time, looking at the ceiling, tossing and turning because I couldn't sleep because there was so much on my mind, and still thinking about all that had happened, my brain just wouldn't shut off.

I was up all hours of the night, flipping the TV channels, walking the floor, looking out of the window, talking to God, or on the computer doing things until I got sleepy enough to go to bed and fall asleep at three or four even 5:00 a.m. I would be gone all day to keep from being at home alone trying to keep from having idle time which would allow me time to think.

Several times while alone I broke down in tears, once I remember all I could do was cry out to God, asking him to help me, I just didn't think I could make it on my own, the pain was just so unbearable for me, it hurt so bad. The pain felt as if it was deeper than I could reach. My uncle said it best at the repast when he said" I can see that the loss of your son has touched your soul".

No matter how I tried, there was still a pain that was unbearable, I had shed so many tears, and it seems to be an endless river of water. I just could not deal with the reality of what had happened.

I can't stop crying
Author Eric A. Hayes
(Step-Brother to Tarrence D. Parks Sr.)
A day of giving thanks, followed by a day of mourning and I'm all cried out. Now I'm no longer a Big Brother,

I'm watching the tears in the eyes of my second mother, and I'm all cried out.

I know that we are all headed down that road, but I didn't think you would get there, not right now, not today. If I had known, I would have had so much more to say. It would have been a repeat of all the conversations before, but I knew I would have said something different this time. Before you walked out the door, made promises that we couldn't keep, and said I'll see you next week at the game. Now I can't stop shaking my head, whenever I say your name.

Do we have to ask why? An answer will not bring my Lil brother back. Tarrence, I miss you already and I just got the call. I pray that you are resting in peace and that we'll continue to praise God through it all. The tears are back now, because I'm remembering the times and how my nephew went from a fatherless night to a fatherless lifetime.

Your death will not be in vain, I know that there is a reason for our sorrow; I prayed that all of those who knew you will change their life-styles before tomorrow. Tomorrow is not promised. I understand that now more than ever before. I thank God for the times we had together and wished that we had no much more…

chapter three
mother's day

MY ONLY CHILD:
Author: Geri Fitzgerald

It seems as though I this is a movie and I can't
　　wake up.
Is this what it feels like when you no longer
　　have a child to parent?
How many children do I have?
He was my ONLY CHILD.

So many times driving and listening to the radio
and a certain song would come on and cause me to
remember him. The tears would begin to rolling
down my face. Out in public, at the store or anywhere,
a thought comes over me relating to him, and tears build
up, many times unable to hold them back, so many
times driving and crying often.

When I'm cooking dinner and realizing that it is one of
his favorite foods. I begin thinking about him and how
he enjoyed food, and now he is gone and not coming

back and will never enjoy these foods again and so often brought tears.

I remember how conscious he was of his appearance; I always said he primped like a woman. There are times that I'm in public and may see a young man who may be dressed similar in style, a clean cut demeanor and the memory of how he took so much time and pride in his appearance.

It was unbelievable how things had to be just right. Sometimes I hear certain music and I remember thinking about special times when he would come over, and how he'd park his car right at the side door and get out, and the way he walked so slow and gentle never getting in a hurry or visualizing him smiling and when he would smile how his smile would light up the room.

All these memories draw so much pain. Then I have to think about the fact that the person that shot my child is still walking the streets, and my grandson is without a father. I know the Lord said vengeance is his, but it still hurts down deep inside, beyond a place to be reached to know that the person that took your child from you, no matter what the age is still walking the streets.

There were so many memories in the beginning when I would replay things in my mind, asking so many questions, questions only a mother would ask. For example, was he afraid at the time of the shooting? Was he in pain? What were his last thoughts? How could someone do something like this? Take another life, someone's child, father, and brother, a nephew. Who gave them the right? This hurts and there is no way to describe how it hurts, the mere thought that someone took the person that you love so much, and in the manner which he was taken, someone took my dreams.

Some of the hardest times for me in the beginning were, days such as **Mother's day**, I remember once thinking and asking myself the question, "**Am I still considered a Mother**?" Now that my only child is gone, I remember when he would call or stop by to bring me that special gift. Now I wait, yet no one comes. I remember crying all day on Mother's Day and days prior, looking at the gifts from past Mother's Days because it was really hard for me.

The first Mother's Day after Tarrence's death was very hard for me I shed many tears because all I could think of was my Son and that he was no longer here, murder unsolved. The memories of other Mother's Days came into my mine making my heart so heavy. My Son was the kind of Son that he bought me something and at some point in that day I would see him, and if he weren't able to buy me something he would be sure to call me and wish me a Happy Mother's Day.

And so, on that first Mother's Day all day the thoughts of all the other Mother's Days and thought of all the different times when he had made his entrance to wish me a Happy Mother's Day or to bring me a gift, or the times when he'd called me to bid me a Happy Mother's Day, sadness came over me tears begin to fall because now I have this thought in mind that some person without the right took my child from me.

So now, when Mother's Day comes I think to myself, this year on Mother's Day he'll neither make a grand entrance with a special gift nor will I hear his voice on the other end of the telephone wishing me a Happy Mother's Day. All I have left are the memories of when he did. And this is all I have now to hold onto and remember forever in my heart are the memories of the many times in the past that my son blessed me with his presence in honoring me for being his mother and sharing his love with me.

I now stop and think to myself, dare I even acknowledge this thing they call Mother's Day now? Because some cruel and heartless person has taken away from me the person that made me a mother, the person that called me ma, the person that confirmed Mother's Day for me is now gone. So again, **dare I celebrate**?

I still often ask myself the question, am I still a mother? I know that I once was, however, the true meaning has been snatched away, and the meaning is absent from my heart, and only pain and sadness exist of what used to be. No child of my own exists anymore to call me and wish me a Happy Mother's Day anymore, no one left to truly acknowledge me as a mother, so again I ask dare I celebrate Mother's Day? The reality of what this day meant is now gone.

> A wife who loses a husband is called a widow.
> A husband who loses a wife is called a widower.
> A child who loses his parents is called an orphan.

But...there is no word for a parent who loses a child?

Author: Anonymous

March 28, 2005: We visited my son's grave for his twenty-ninth birthday and remembered him; by wearing special pictured T-shirts and then going to dinner we ate his favorite food that day "pizza." We also each released a balloon in his honor and shared a word about him as the balloons launched.

June 21, 2005: We visited Tarrence on Father's Day I took his son to leave a wreath for him. We often visit him on special days, clean his headstone and leave flowers as a token of our love and remembrance. Holidays were times he looked forward to spending with family and eating good food.

I remember the first year after my son was murdered my hair began to break and I began to lose weight because of my nerves. I was trying to stay busy to keep myself occupied; often I realized that I had gone through the day without eating, so I began to lose weight. Thank God for my neighbor Mrs. Robinson, she is the true spirit of a Christian. She called me every day to see how I was doing, she fed us dinner, checked to see if I needed anything from the store, and she would come over and sit down and talk with me.

During this time you truly find out who truly cares and who your friends truly are by what they do for you I had a couple that kept in touch daily calling me to make sure I was all right. One friend called me especially during the times when she knew it was hard for me, such as my son's birthday, Christmas, and the first anniversary of his death. Another friend called often from out of town to see how my mental and physical state was, she tried to encourage other forms of help.

These kinds of friends are rare and sent truly by God. This is a time when you find out that those friends that you would move heaven and earth to support might not do the same for you. During this time was a learning experience for me also.

I remember the first Christmas was so hard for us getting together without Tarrence, we opened our gifts thinking of him and missing him and we all cried hugged together because it was so painful without his presence. Also this was the first Christmas my sister in law had celebrated without her mother who had died two weeks prior to Tarrence. It started out so sad but we got through it together by the grace of God.

There is not a day that goes by that I don't think of my child many times in the course of that day, there are many times, that I still think of him and shed tears at the thought of him being gone, I am trying to grasp the concept that he is truly gone.

The hardest part is when you know that your child is gone and won't be back, death is such a life altering experience your days will never be the same again. I will never enjoy another holiday the same, because I will always be reminded that he was taken from us during that holiday and won't be with you. It will never be as happy as it once was, because it will always be missing that one person, that special piece that made the puzzle complete is now gone. This to me is like a confirmation or a wakeup call or a slap in the face reminder that Tarrence is no longer with us.

There were many times when my grandson would ask me, Grandma did the Police find the bad man that killed my dada yet? And he would actually pray asking God to help the police find the person(s). I have always believed that God sees further down the road than we do, I believe that God put things into place relating to my son's death down to the people who would see him alive that last time, I believe that God knew it would be our last time with him, that is why as I think back on that night things were just so perfect yet unusual.

I believe that it was meant by God that my grandson be in my life upon my son's demise. I truly believe that I would not have made it had it not been for him being in my life. Although my family has relied on each other for strength, it is my grandson that kept me moving forward and focused. There were many times when I know and felt like I could have easily balled up and given up. Because I had to care for my grandson this kept me moving and busy.

I remember my grandson had watched me cry so frequently that when my son's name was mentioned he would look at me or even touch me under my eyes to make sure I wasn't crying. I remember a few times when he caught me in one of my crying moments he told me, "grandma it's going to be all right". And I knew it would it just seemed as though that Joy often spoken of that was supposed to come in the morning was taking so long to come for me. As I sit here, crying I think back to the days when I would ask God when the pain would stop hurting.

I often have moments when thoughts or memories will come over me and I begin to cry or late at night sometimes or when memories comes to mind and the tears begin to roll down my cheeks. Or upon hearing of another young person being killed or seeing someone shot especially in the head it takes me back to my son's death and it rehashes the pain all over again.

It's like my mom and I say to each other, a year has gone by so fast and it seems as though we take steps to move forward, a memory or something comes right along and takes us back to square one and the pain is once again as vivid as it was on November 25th 2005 and we relive it all over again, leaving us to wonder will Joy ever come in the morning for us? I know that God promises that it will and I hold to his word waiting for that moment of joy, when the pain won't hurt so much, and Tarrence's memories will bring a smile instead of tears.

As of this moment we still one year later, sometimes I can't muster up the words to talk about him, when something is asked.

About a year after Tarrence's murder I visited a support group called MOMS and during the meeting, was asked to share if I could what happened as the new member and I was so overcome with grief when asked if I wanted to talk about it that all I could do was cry for about ten minutes.

So in my opinion and from my experience grief is

many emotions rolled up together. I believe that each person experiences grief in very similar ways, however, I believe that each person deals with it in his or her own way. No two people deal with the loss of a loved one in the same way. Some choose to hold it in while others prefer after a while to talk about it and share it, which is good because you release the stress of the pain that you have encountered by sharing it with others, and I believe you get stronger.

I am a living witness that you do have a hard time moving on, and letting go of the past. People need counseling or other types of help to get past the grief and death of a loved one. It is truly a traumatic experience in our lives. It is a time when you have to accept a great loss, the change that now exist in your life and you have to adapt to those changes accepting that someone that was once here is no longer due to illness or some type of traumatic experience that has taken them out of your life. I believe that this is something that takes time to absorb and adjust to, and I know that it is a, day-by-day process, and with continuous Prayer and faith God will see you through.

You have to know that it's okay to cry when the urge comes over you. A Mother, child, spouse, father, sister, brother and others are very important family members to lose. Do not to go on without some type of mourning/ grief. Some people do bounce back faster than others. Because they are stronger and accept the loss better, not that they love them any less.

March 28th 2006: Today is the 29th Birthday of my only son my family and I went to spend time with him.

We took flowers, balloons, pictures, and my oldest niece brought him a special drink because his birthday was important to him, Tarrence loved celebrating his birthday. I wish we were there visiting someone else and not him, it still seems like a bad dream, yet the reality is apparent in the day to day routine. He is on my mind often, and in my heart daily, his memories will forever be imprinted in my heart and mind.

Not realizing that the quick act of violence would impact so many lives or break so many hearts, this vicious act has taken a son, father, cousin, nephew, grandson, special friend, and brother a descent living individual that had the right to live as everyone else did.

How dare this person choose to take another life? Who gave this person the right? And as a lesson of this death and many like his remember that tomorrow is not promised to us and that we should love and acknowledge those we love while they are here for we know not the time, day or hour that they will be taken away from us, and we may not get another chance to share with them what we feel.

When a parent dies, you lose your past; when a child dies, you lose your future.

I sat one day reading a story about Christina Applegate, and she talked about how the birth of her daughter had saved her life because of many things she had gone through in her life during that time. Something she said I thought was so awesome was that when her daughter was born as she laid her eyes on her, she thought she was the most beautiful thing ever, she said that as she looked at her daughter she felt her heart open up and wrap itself around her. I thought to myself what a wonderful expression of the feeling the birth of a child gives a mother and then I thought to myself the pain is the equal opposite to lose a child.

Parental Grief
Author: Unknown

It is frequently said that the grief of bereaved parents is the most intense grief known. When a child dies, parents feel that a part of them has died, that a vital and core part of them has been ripped away. Bereaved parents indeed do feel that the death of their child is "the ultimate deprivation" The grief caused by their child's death is not only painful but profoundly disorienting-children are not supposed to die.

chapter four
reflection around the crime

**The Death of a Child, the Grief of the Parents: A
Lifetime Journey**.

hildren are not supposed to die... Parents expect
to see their children grow and mature. Ultimately,
parents expect to die and leave their children
behind. The death of a child signifies the loss of the
future, of hopes and dream. By Arnold and Gemma
1994

May 16, 2006: I am sitting here today absorbing all
that has happened in the past few days. My family and
I were just back on May 10, 2006 from a long needed
vacation. While on vacation a drug bust occurred in
The Square, the area in which my son had once lived
and was murdered. We received several calls to let us
know what was happening. Oddly, we had gotten more
information and updates from friends "in the streets"
than from our friends the "Chicago Police Department,"

who vow to serve and protect and promised to keep us informed.

Apparently in the square, the FEDS/Chicago Police had been watching for two years since January 2004, until the drug bust of a family called the Coven's drug ring on May 9, 2006. I also came upon documents from a family friend relating to this FBI investigation, which shed yet more light on this situation regarding the drug bust. In this over one hundred page document My Son's murder is discussed between two men, who were arrested as they mentioned Tarrence as a rival threat to someone.

The Square is an area where mostly low-income families reside in buildings that resemble a small version of the projects. Located in a part of town toward the lower west-side of Chicago called K-Town. It is has a visual of a lower class area, not maintained, where many don't care about others. I have heard many say that it is an area where they will sell their mother for drugs. It's a known drug area, high crime and should be a constant police beat. I would imagine some live there because they have nowhere else to go, it is an area of subsidized housing for low income families, however others use it as a place to do unlawful things that they know they would not get away with in other areas.

One account that we've been told about was that he was set up because he had conflict with a young man from the square believed to be one of the Covens family members, he was lured over there by so called friends to be killed. One of the Covens' I'm told had threatened him and told him to stay out of the Square, which is where he once lived with a girl friend and that is why he was killed, because he wouldn't let them dictate to him where he could or couldn't go.

Tarrence had once told me that a gun had been pulled on him and he had been told to stay from over there. He was one of those young men who was strong headed and had often told me he felt he should be able to go wherever he wanted to. Unfortunately trusting the wrong people, being stubborn, and having people around him that he thought were his friends, this cost him his life.

We were told, he was supposed to have gone over to visit a female friend on that dreaded night, but he was ambushed in the process. We have been told several stories from robbery, random shooting, but we will never truly know the truth. Only the people involved and God know the truth. God will see justice for us in his time.

The story was also that he had received a phone call that night from this female friend, which is why he was in the area that night. We were told that Tarrence also made a phone call prior to his arrival directing someone to open the door, not knowing what was said following his request. We were told that upon arrival in the Square Tarrence exited his car and began to walk toward the building in the Square where this female lived, the friend he was with said the shooting began as he began to run to catch up to Tarrence. It seems that they were ambushed, and only **cowards** do this type of thing. This sounds to have been the making of a set-up.

The question that nags me is who did he speak with that may have shared information with the shooter(s)? That led him to be set up? If this was the case, AMBUSHED is what happened to Tarrence and the friend with him, using that visit as a means to get him there knowing he would go because he knew and trusted them without question of loyalty as friends, and the fact that he had once lived among them. However there apparently was no loyalty, and he should not have trusted them.

We were also told that a white blazer came out of nowhere to assist in getting my son's wounded body to an ambulance that was conveniently sitting at a corner (which never happens in that part of town). It was there that police put him in a squad car and said he sat there for roughly what seemed to be about half an hour, dying before the ambulance began any work on him, we are told that the police even attempted to question him before assisting him medically and getting him to the hospital, which possibly cost him his life.

Why did they stick him in a squad car and let him sit? Why would they try to question a person who apparently was severely wounded in the head, and knowingly could not answer any questions? Were they more concerned about hurting their case rather than saving a life? Is a life not worth more than a case? Why did the surveillance team(s), (Feds/Chicago Police Officer's) not do something to try to avoid this apparent ambush, if they knew of it from the surveillance and telephone taps? I feel that they sacrificed a life, my son's life" to protect their case, that is what it appears to me. Is that what they feel about us as people? African Americans, Minority, Human beings. Is a human life worth so little to them that they would jeopardize a life for a case?

I am convinced that they knew this incident was to occur, because they had access to conversations of those they had surveiled, according to the documents I read. I saw no documented evidence that anyone tried to prevent the shooting of my son therefore allowing this to happen, other than the mysterious white blazer that appeared from nowhere. This compromise has shaken the mere foundation of a descent, loving, respectable, hardworking, and tax-paying family in that this incident took the life of someone's child, someone's father and loved one.

I feel as though somewhere down the line these officials should be held accountable for to have allowed a life to be lost to avoid jeopardizing a case with the drug family targets. This makes them no better than the bad guy, this was an example of how they value the lives of citizens. They have sworn to SERVE & PROTECT not kill or allow to be killed.

In my opinion these officials tarnish the badges and the sworn oath taken by many of the things they allowed to happen this night. And while they were undercover portraying themselves to be dirty cops/drug dealers or whomever they perpetrated, I believe that they fell victim to what they perpetrated, "Dirty Cops." They allowed the life of a citizen to be compromised on the night of November 25th 2005, on the West Side of Chicago, defying what they are sworn to do, "protect life" in my opinion they without a doubt in breach of their duty. They compromised a life for a case, something I feel to be an inhumane act especially for a police official sworn to serve, protect and save lives.

I often think about these and so many other things and it hurts me that my son died this way, with Policeman and Government officials right there and he still lost his life because I believe they chose **not** to jeopardize their case, yet to let his life be lost instead.

The Chicago Police did tell us that a drug war was going on over territory, the newspaper article claims Tarrence was killed because he was a rival, there were no drugs found on my son, nor in the possession of his car when searched before being returned to us. That tells me that the night he was killed he was not over there in any negative capacity and that there may be some truth to one of the many stories we've heard about Tarrence being set-up.

There are so many details, lies, stories; it hurts to think of the Bull _____ involved in my son's death that to me meant not a hill of beans in reference to him losing his life over.

We never found the jacket Tarrence wore the night he was shot, which had been a birthday gift from his girl friend. His friend said he had his jacket on when he was put into the ambulance, which was no-where to be found according to the hospital upon release of his belongings.

The hospital claims it was destroyed but I don't believe that story because we received everything else and nothing else had blood on it that would make it necessary to be destroyed. I believe his jacket was stolen from him while he lay in the hospital fighting for the life he would lose.

The ambulance personnel claim his jacket and personal property was transferred with him to the hospital's emergency room. In spite of it all, I know that there is a God and he sits high and looks low at all of us and the things we do. And all of us will be accountable in his eyes.

For the wrong we do to our fellowman with that being said it helps my heart to know that **ALL** those who contributed to my son's death, playing any part in it, even those who had the opportunity to prevent it and did not, have sinned in the eyes of God. They too will be judged for their role in allowing a life to be taken thereby creating a sin before God.

"For we know him who said, "It is mine to avenge; I will repay," and again, "The LORD will judge his people" Hebrews 10:30

By no means does this erase the heartache that dwells in my heart. I now have to go the cemetery and look at a tombstone when I want to see my son. I no longer have the ability to hold him, kiss him, hear his voice or look into his eyes anymore. On Mother's day I didn't get that call that I used to get. And on the holidays he won't walk in kissing everyone.

December 26, 2006: Yes, it's been one year, since my son was taken from me and so many days I look at his picture and just can't believe that he is gone, the tears stream down my face and I stare in disbelief. And then I think to myself how could someone take him from me? And the pain sends a rush through my body as though it were a slap to my face. Just thinking about the way my son died in the streets, never knowing what happened. He left home expecting to be here on earth a while longer, to see his son and his family.

I re-live so many different instances each and every day. On the outside I appear to be this calm person, while all the while on the inside my heart has inside an indescribable sadness that seems to reach my soul, and I feel as though I can't get pass the sadness and the thought that my son is no longer with me, especially when I look at his pictures with his son so full of love and it saddens my heart.

What **hurts** most: These things bring sadness and tears;

- The thought that he is gone, never to come back, never to be able to see his face, touch him or hear his voice again. Watch him enjoy time with his family.

- The way he died, no closure, no answers and the way the police handled it.

- No one in custody, just another case still open

- His son growing up without him and asking me questions like, "Did they catch the person that shot my dad?" Or telling me he doesn't want to forget his dad's voice, how he looked, walked or smiled. Or that if he had one wish it would be that his dad was alive again.

- The way someone would be so heartless to steal from him as he lay fighting for his life, in a place whose purpose is to save lives.

- Having to go to the cemetery to visit my only child who left this earth before me. And knowing the many things I will never see him do.

His best friend married the summer of 2006, and I remembered crying all the way to the wedding thinking about the fact that I would never see a wedding day for my son, will never share with him his first apartment, and so many first things that you look forward to seeing or sharing with your child. I then thanked God for his only child, a son.

I remember visiting my son's grave a day prior to the wedding of his good friend and talking to him saying, well your guy (best friend) is getting married tomorrow and I so hate that you will not be there to share in the happy occasion.

His friend and I had talked prior to the wedding and he was so sad at the thought that Tarrence would not share this day with him, because he said Tarrence was the person that he had envisioned standing beside him as he made this important step in his life. He credited Tarrence for encouraging him to stay with his children's mother so they would have both parents, and Tarrence wasn't there to see this moment transpire.

And again, I thought neither will I ever share in such

a happy occasion on his behalf, because someone has cheated us both of that opportunity. There were special moments at the wedding that I thought about Tarrence and tears welled up thinking about his jovial spirit and how he might have responded in certain circumstances during the wedding, with laughter, or a giggle, such as the groom "his best friend" getting the garter from under the new wife's dress or catching it when it was thrown, or standing on the wall because he wasn't a dancer at all.

January 16, 2007, A little over a year has come and gone and yet the pain of losing my son is still so fresh. Yes, I go through the day doing the many things that need to be done, though constantly he is on my mind, so often tears well up in my eyes because something may bring a memory, causing me to feel the emotions of remembering that he is no longer with us. Often I think of the way he died and feel that it is oh so unfair because he was a good person with such a good and kind heart and he didn't deserve to die in the street as he did.

Yes I still often think of many other things that will never happen now that he is gone such as more children one day, meeting that special person and getting his own place which was some of his last conversation, and dinner with him, or seeing him come through that door on a normal day or one of his special holidays like Christmas of July 4th. He loved Christmas because he enjoyed the feeling of giving and enjoyed the expressions of his son receiving from him, and I think it was gratifying for him as well.

What he didn't realize is that I would trade all the gifts

in the world to have the gift of him here again and being able to see his face, touch him, hug him, hear his voice, or allow his son to hear him call his name or mine again. Or just to see him stand there in the doorway or drive up in the drive again, that would be OH such a wonderful thing!

I think of him each time we sit down especially during holidays or when I cook his favorite foods. But yes I go thru the days with him in my thoughts going through the motions of trying to live as close to a normal life as possible after losing my only child and trying to balance the pain while the person that took his life is still out there somewhere walking, living and seeing his family.

We are left to deal with the void, that person's actions caused to our family, friends and others. My heart and life are forever changed, and it's as if a piece of my life has been turned off. They say that your eyes are the window to your soul, well my face has a smile but within my eyes there is a sadness that reflect the pain that dwells deep within because of the loss of my son, I feel the sadness that dwells within my eyes and my heart, and it seems to be a pain and sadness that will never go away, a sadness that seems to run deeper than I can reach, seeming to have no end.

Tarrence didn't live at home so I didn't see him regularly, but I saw him often and when I wanted or needed to hear his voice or check on him I had the ability to call him or see him at my mom's house occasionally. Or his surprise visits to see his son were always a highlight to us both.

I had always thought of myself as being a good Christian as much as I could be, I have faith in God, and with the murder of my son, my faith was truly tested. For a short time I didn't go to church. I felt the desire to be to myself at first. When I first went back I found it really hard for me to praise God. I would, but then in the back of my mind there was this other voice that was saying, why, should you be saying God is good and your son is dead. Because he was gone, I felt guilt for being thankful or happy. I felt as though I was betraying my son in some way, the guilt for being thankful or happy, feeling I shouldn't be because he is gone.

I had been off work for some time now, lost my only child and then in the back of my mind this voice would say. "Why is God so good?" He allowed you to lose your only child, "Should you be praising him?" I found it to be a struggle but I kept going to church and once I started back it did get better. And what I learned out of that and some of the many messages that my Pastor taught on Sunday, was that often God tests our faith, we don't know how or why but he does.

Facing Forever What We Have Lost
By: Kate Convissor
Suddenly we have joined a select Community, one we had never thought to enter.
We are sisters of sorrow and void. Suddenly or identity linked to what we have lost.
Can this be? We laugh again; but it is a different life, the loss is not recovered from, not "gotten over

chapter five
support in a time of grief

"MOMS" Mother's of Murdered Sons

my pastor once said God knows that it's easy for us to jump up and praise God when things are going well for us. But the test is when things aren't going well, this too is when God wants us to praise him, in the good times as well as in the bad, and it's often found that when we are doing bad it's difficult to praise God if at all, because this is when the faith may falter or we stumble and lose sight that he knows all about what we are going through and will see us through it if we just trust him. I now am a living witness of this message, but I know that, "All things work together for the good of them who love the Lord

"All things are possible if you trust God" {Luke 18:27}

January 22, 2007: And no contact at all, we have had to stay in touch with Chicago's finest - yeah right! They have actually gotten to the point where they are not even returning my calls at all. It hurts me because they seem to have moved on to the next case with no respect of any type of closure or information to the parents/family of the person. But my question to them is what if it was you? Wouldn't you want to be treated in a better manner and given the courtesy of being informed about what if anything is going on with the case?

One year later and emotionally it's better to a degree; we are able to talk more often without "so many tears" as Tupac said in his song. However we continue to hurt, there is sadness in my heart that I honestly don't believe will ever go away, a void never to be filled. A longing that will never be satisfied, that longing is the longing to see my child's face again, hear his voice, hold him and tell him love you. But you see this will never take place because someone took it upon themselves to take my child's life for some unknown reason, as if they were God.

I once tried contacting the FBI Agent who headed the raid in the area where my son was killed and left two messages and I did briefly speak to two agents, one of who gave me contact information for a Policeman affiliated with the case to get information. One of my questions was will the young men arrested be charged relating to my son's murder? The answer was no, FBI would be prosecuting for drugs. I was told to speak with the local authorities relating to other charges.

I called this special agent and spoke briefly to him, I was told by him that he would return my call but I have not received a call to this day. One of the things the Officer told me that was assigned to Tarrence's case was that as soon as they found out anything, they would call us into the office and sit us down to explain it to us. They never kept their promise to call us nor have they ever told us anything useful or helpful pertaining to the case. In fact they stopped returning our calls about the case.

January 2007: I had begun taking Tarrence Jr. to the library to learn how to check out books, use the computer, and to show him the many advantages at the library. While there I noticed literature about a Support Group and I took the literature. It was about a support group relating to grief and the loss of a child. I thought to myself maybe this is something that will help me because I still cried a lot and my mind was still so restless. I left a message and the founder Phyllis Duncan returned my call, and I visited the very next meeting.

I was so nervous thinking what if I start to cry and many other things came to mind about going to this meeting. I had gotten to a point that if it wasn't family or close friends I didn't want to interact at all, out of an inverted feeling I now had, feeling the desire to be left alone.

Well I sat down and Phyllis began the meeting in Prayer, everyone introduced themselves, my turn came and she asked if I wanted to share my story about what had brought me to be in this place. Well, I thought I was strong enough to at least talk about what happened, but oh my God! As I tried to begin my introduction it was as though the flood gate of a river had opened up, tears fell from everywhere and I couldn't stop the tears from falling, the more I wiped the more tears fell.

I remember Phyllis and some of the other ladies in the group telling me its okay, we understand, take your time. It gave me comfort knowing that these women understood my hurt, my pain, they didn't judge me for breaking down in public, they comforted and consoled me, they knew what to expect, and they respected my emotional state.

As I listened to the stories of other women, I realized I had something in common with them. Many of the women had lost a son to murder and like me suffering from the lost of a child. After that Saturday I became a faithful member of "MOMS" – Mother's of Murdered Sons, a support group that meets the second Saturday of the month at the Bellwood Library. It's a group of mothers whose sons have been murdered looking for answers to emotions, comfort, understanding and support.

It's such a hurting experience to see other's hurt in the same way that you do because you relate to the pain and suffering that they endure in such a similar way. The sad thing is that you re-live the hurt over and over again, each time a new mother comes into the group because you know the hurt and pain that they are going through.

Many times we discuss the anger of not knowing anything about the person that killed our children. We are frustrated because the police apparently don't care and are not doing anything, so your concerns go unaddressed. I thank God for MOMS because it gave me the support I needed and the courage to re-enter the world, and to begin getting pass the pain of losing my son. I thank my family and other women who have experienced what I have, we help each other to get through it.

January 24, 2007: The pain is still so fresh; there is not a day that goes by that I don't think of my son in some way. Remembering how he died, why, where, and the way the police and FBI handled the case. Unfair and just disrespectful as a human it seems to me. I often glance at my son's picture still in disbelief that he is gone, I guess still trying to digest the actual thought of it all and try to rationalize it, and then the tears begin to gather in my eyes because at that moment it hits me that he is no longer here with us and the pain and hurt rushes through my body as the blood does in my veins. I then begin to think to myself about all the many things that he will miss, his son will grow up without a father and the last special event he shared with his son was his kindergarten graduation months before his murder in June 2005. My son will never have any more children, that is it for me I will never have anymore maternal grandchildren. Only the one's with my husband's son and his wife, which I am very thankful for also.

There are many times I think back on the different things Tarrence did when he would come over. One of the first things he'd always get a bottle of water out of the refrigerator. Memories of what was are all that are left for us: his car, pictures, various documents are all that suggest he has passed through and left a loving spirit and footprints of love on the hearts of those who loved him.

Foot Prints and Memories:

Author: Unknown

It's funny how someone can come in and out of your life so quickly, yet leave footprints and memories in your heart forever.

We are attempting to move on with our lives because we don't have a choice in the matter; no matter how unfair we may feel about his death we try to go on. With a heavy heart that carries the memories implanted in my heart and mind, never to forget every detail and thought of his brief twenty-eight years of life gone in the blink of an eye.

He was with us Thanksgiving and then the next day he was taken away from us, all I had to hold on to was yesterday's memories. If I had one thing to tell anyone, that would be to love your family and don't take for granted, there may not be a tomorrow it is not promise.

Life is so short and as the Bible tells us we know not the hour or the time of day. So don't be afraid to love and let those you love know it. Be happy and live life doing what you enjoy. Don't let anyone cheat you out of the time you have here on earth because that time is so precious and we don't know how much of it we have with each other.

I thank God for bringing me through this very difficult time in life. I must admit it was THE toughest battle yet we endured as a family. He gave us the strength that we needed to get through each day and it was day by day that we made it by God's grace and mercy. He gave us peace in our hearts and minds and most of all he gave us each other to lean on when times were so hard that we could hardly get through the days that lie ahead. This was truly the time I know there was only one set of footprints in the sand because it is the time that God carried me.

Foot Prints

Author: Unknown

I noticed that many times along the path of life there was only one set of footprints. I also noticed that it happened at the very lowest and saddest times in my life. The Lord replied, "Precious child," I love you and I would never leave you. During your trial and suffering, when you see only one set of footprints, it was then that I carried you."

I often used to wonder what could be so bad to make a person want to give up on life and want to go on forgetting about family, until the murder of my son. With the grief and pain endured, which has been the most difficult days ever, after my son was murdered I understand all too well how people lose that desire to go on after losing a child or a loved one so close to them. I now know where that desire comes from and how it feels to want to give up on life and not to really care about anything because if it were not for the Lord I don't know where I would be.

Unemployed during this time, I had lots of time on my hands and nothing to do, this helped me to see that I could have easily rolled up in my bed and just gave up because I was hurting so deeply inside. My heart had broken into a million pieces, and I just could not accept how Tarrence was gone so quickly and I had just seen him.

I felt that all I wanted to do was lie in the bed, thinking about how I couldn't believe he was gone and thinking to myself, this couldn't be true, it still seemed so much like a bad dream, I would replay the days that began that nightmare, reliving it over and over again. But God left me a beautiful grandson that is in my care and he is what kept me. As the song title reads: I need you to survive, I now have him to care for, he too was worried and watching my every move, watching for tears. With the help of God I knew that I could make it.

Whenever he would hear his dads name mentioned because he had seen the many tears in the past he knew what usually came next, I knew too that he was going through his own grieving and I wanted to try to be strong for him, which is something I'd lost sight of in the midst of my own grief. I remember when I had to tell Tarrence Jr. that his dad was gone he got the strangest look on his face of anger, pounding his fist into his other hand, he stormed out of the kitchen into his room where he lay and cried. My youngest niece Briana was also over and she tried to comfort him, telling him it would be ok. That was another moment I would have given anything not to experience.

I signed him up for counseling at school so that he would have an outlet outside of family. He asked many questions as he still does and I have tried to answer them as best I can. As time has progressed it has gotten somewhat better for us; we can now most of the time talk about Tarrence without the tears most of the time. Although sometimes the tears do come with the mention of his name, or a thought I still hurt when I visit the cemetery, still thinking I can't believe he is here; and Tarrence Jr. usually goes with him we are better.

Many people don't go to the cemetery after the funeral for many reasons I sometimes go when I feel the need for closeness or a talk with him. In an odd way, going there I feel closer; it is my way of letting him know that I have not forgotten him.

I know that only the shell of his body is in the grave none the less that is where they laid him, and I know that his spirit is free and his soul is happy, no more pain or frustrations of the world. The only pain is ours in missing him, because he is no longer with us.

When I think about where we are and where we have come from, I am reminded of a song that was very popular, because the Artist also lost his wife to cancer, and his song is my testimony. The name of the song is "I never would have made it" by Artist, Marvin Sapp.

chapter six
remembering my son

March 23, 2007: Almost the second birthday since Tarrence's death and he would have been Thirty yrs old. It has been almost two years since the death of my son and I still think of him often. So many things still draw instant tears, so many things bring sadness within my heart when I see or hear them. I miss hearing some of the many things he'd say, such as when he called me Ma' or to check on his son, saying "Ma where's my baby?"

When I drive through the Austin area he instantly fills my heart. I also still see his car sitting there in the front of my mom's house and him coming in the door or ringing the bell when he forgot his key. I can still see him preparing to change clothes and how he took so long, I think of how precious his son and family was to him and how protective he was of his son.

While I believe that everything is in God's hands and

he makes no mistakes, this is just something that is so hard and truly a test to accept and digest. I wish within my heart that there had been another way, but I know that God knew things we didn't.

There are songs that I hear that make me reflect back on him sung by artists like Yolanda Adams song: Be blessed & The Battle is not yours. Because he was going through some things that he needed God to help him through. Society had been hard on him "so hard" it wouldn't give him a chance to prove how productive and positive he could be as a citizen with steady work. Each time he got a job, it would never last as he hoped.

It's funny how many people will do anything to become a part of the American dream and to get a piece of the pie. But those who are born bred and live here all their lives can't even get a break. It's a sad thing the bureaucracy, Politics and red tape involved in just getting a break. To get a job, after even a slight tarnish on your background you are never forgiven by the system and society. You are thrown aside rather than rehabilitated or helped.

March 28, 2007: A sunny day, windy with a chill. We went to the Cemetery as we've done since Tarrence's murder to acknowledge his Birthday. Before we left we launched balloons, Tarrence Jr. wanted to launch last and he did. He and I both had included notes to the ribbon ends of our balloons, and upon Tarrence Jr. releasing his balloon he said Happy Birthday da da, I love you and I miss you a lot. As his balloon began to lift into the air it wedged between branches in a tree and he was so disappointed, feeling that his dad wouldn't get his balloon. I told him, tell your dad to get his balloon from the tree. Lil Tarrence said da da get your birthday balloon, and it was such an amazing moment because as he said it, seconds later the balloon released and lifted up into the air and began to climb into the air and to Tarrence Jr. that was such an amazing, moment, his da da had heard him talk to him.

We at that moment also felt such a sense of spiritual bliss to see this special moment because it was apparent that it had brought such delight to Tarrence Jr. The moment repeated itself with my niece Briana; to the children it seemed to be again confirmation of spiritual interaction with the person they had lost. It was a heartwarming feeling to see the delight on their faces as things came together at the right moment.

June 21, 2007: As Father's Day gets closer the thought that my son is no longer here weighs heavy on my mind and in my heart. I think often of my grandson who lives with only the memory of his father, whom he had such a short time with. Yet it could have been worse he could not have ever met his father yet God blessed him to be with him for six years before taking him.

As I search in the files I come across a letter written to me once when my son was in jail for 2-3 months. The letter expressed how he never thought he would be sitting in jail and he was thinking of all the things that I had tried to warn him about in this tough life to stay away from. He said that he couldn't believe that he was sitting in the very spot he thought he'd never sit in.

Tarrence talked about changes he would make upon being released, the things he would do differently to make life better for himself. He talked about how life was so hard for young black men, when they have any type of case against them. He said society is responsible for pushing him into the many situations and though they make the ultimate mistake, society and the system never lets them forget their mistakes, and as a result of that mistake you can't find jobs.

The police forever harass them especially in certain areas when you are a minority. And even though you go to jail and do your time you are forever sentenced, that mistake you made is never forgiven and you aren't allowed to forget it even though you try hard to live right.

It is almost like in the Biblical days with talk of the lepers and how they were social outcasts, it's the same type of situation. They say you go to jail to pay your debt to society however the system is set up that you never finish paying your debt.

You can't find a job because of your background and the question asked on the application, when you are honest they won't hire you and they tell you if you lie that's grounds for termination. How do you rise above the old lifestyle and put it behind you, when society doesn't give you a chance to do better or to prove that you want to?

And they wonder why the cycle of young black men returning to jail is so high. Men need to make a living, they need to eat. Many of them have families to feed. How are they supposed to provide for themselves and their families? If not given the opportunity to make an honest dollar and to prove that they can again be productive in society after incarceration. What else is there for them to do? They deserve the opportunity to make their contribution, without looking over their shoulder, to be proud, and to have integrity in what they do to better themselves and to truly be counted as men.

As I read his letter, tears rolled down my face because I understood what he was saying. I see it every day, and I know that he was truly trying to find another job after being laid off with no success. I saw the pride he had and how he enjoyed working, buying clothes for his son without having to be told or asked. You could see the sense of pride in his having a job had given him even though the job only paid $8 hour, which isn't a lot of money.

I believe that the government needs to work harder to continue to raise the wage to a descent salary to live on. We have people living in shelters who work every day because they don't make enough on that minimum wage job to meet the expenses that come with an apartment and often to pay the rent.

The reason we have drug dealers on the corners is because there are no jobs, no way to make money, no one willing to give them a break, no guidance, and for some yes no parental involvement. There are truly some young men who long for a chance to start over, but never get that chance. I think that many of the black men are misunderstood, need opportunity and many of them need guidance, and many come from homes where there was none.

Among many other things you have some that have raised themselves because they had no father figure. Some mothers are either too busy trying to pay the bills, leaving the kid unattended, allowing the streets to raise them or trying to still get her own groove on. This leaves no allowance for structure, discipline, guidance, love, compassion and understanding. These things are important to a child in order to come up as a descent productive individual. Without it, many of them are lost and doomed to life in the streets or jail.

I remember being a single mother, often working overtime trying to make enough money to pay the bills, still being unable to afford them activities to keep them busy and out of the streets. I did not spend enough time with my son. If you don't watch it they will find gangs or others that will give them the time they so desperately seek and need but lack in the home They get involved with the street gangs because they have this false belief that they care and have their back, not realizing it's a road that leads only to jail or death.

chapter seven
life is precious

i often think about the day it all happened and wonder what his last thoughts might have been, was he in pain? Was he afraid? Or was it quick? Then I wonder how someone could be so cold as to take another life? Did they have a conscious? Apparently not, they did it. I wonder if he had not been where he was if he would still be alive today?

I think about the last time I saw my son and think about had I known it would be my last time with him what I would have done differently. I often replay that last Thanksgiving dinner before his murder, the family picture taken that night, and I am happy that he was with family that last time, and that it had to be an act of God to bring us all together before his final date, though I can't help wishing that he would have had just a little more time and wondering why he had to go like he did?

As I think about these moments tears begin to roll down my face, sadness and pain fill my heart. Thinking about how my son was gone so fast. And Stevie Wonder's song, "These three words" say it perfectly, how someone can be taken in the twinkle of an eye, so love each other today.

I live everyday with the thought of my son's murder, no one arrested, no closure, knowing that it is a reality that he is gone to never return, yet in another way I struggle still after almost two years still trying to accept and digest the fact that he is gone and won't return, it still seems so much like a dream that I would love to wake up from. With a pain that is indescribable, and a sadness that reaches deeper than you ever thought something could reach, it's like an emptiness that you can't seem to fill.

You wonder how you can go on because it seems as though your world has stopped, and you can't seem to get back on the ride of life, no energy, no desire, because of the disbelief of what has happened. And it's something that no one can really help you with, it's something that only you & God can tackle together, and the only way to succeed is by **having the will** to do it, otherwise you will lose the fight.

It's strange how losing a loved one brings such grief and sadness, it seems different yet immeasurable when it is your child vs. a Mother or Father you know that you love them too but it seems that to lose a child damages you so much deeper. I am thankful to still have my mother, who once lost a daughter as a toddler. I now understand what she went through to some degree having walked in her shoes though my loss was to murder. My sister died as a toddler due to sickness.

I lost my father and grandparents to sickness also. Somehow losing my only child, that son seems as though it cut to the very core of my being. You want to ball up and waste away, crying your eyes out, because as someone once said it seems as though your heart has been ripped from your chest and no one understands, no one can help you, no one can relieve that horrible excruciating pain that exists.

There's one thing that losing my son has given me if nothing else and that is a different understanding for the loss of a child. There is nothing like knowing what a person is going through, than to have gone through it for yourself. When I see or hear of a murder or death now, especially of a child, I say a prayer for that family, and I get sadness in my heart all over again because, I have as they say "walked a mile in their shoes."

When I hear of a murder of a young man especially I find myself caught up in the emotions of the story and when I realize it, tears are rolling down my face, because I'm equating the feelings of the hurt, pain and sadness of losing Tarrence, yet compassion for the family and the person because. I know what they must be going through as I have experienced and I wonder WILL THE MURDERS EVER END?

November and December 2007: The Holidays seem to be harder for me this time for some reason, when I listen to holiday songs and they make me sad because they are a reminder Tarrence was taken during this time. This time or year also serves as a reality check in the sense that it reminds me that he actually is no longer here when Thanksgiving comes and goes because he never came over because he would always come whenever we cooked because he loved to eat.

I still have a special spot set up at my table for Tarrence because it is the spot he sat on the last holiday dinner with us, so my family respects that spot when we get together and Tarrence Jr. wrote a note that reads "No one sits here." Although he's not there that's his special spot. Tarrence Jr. as he gets older talks more of his dad.

On Thanksgiving at dinner time we usually hold hands around the table to say grace before we eat, with each person saying one thing they are thankful for. December 2007, Christmas day it's about 7a.m. Tarrence Jr. runs in the bedroom standing up in the bed he says, All who misses my dad raise your hand. And all who misses seeing him raise your hand. We raised our hands again and we all shared a hug together.

This I guess was his way of letting us know that he was missing his dad especially on Christmas.

Dinner time came and we were about to say grace, and Tarrence Jr. who usually never wants to say anything, with nerves built up whispers to me. Let's say the prayer that we say at Thanksgiving, we gathered around the table to each gave thanks for something, and when it was Tarrence's turn he said, I thank God for my dada and the time he had with me and I am thankful for my family, he then got the strangest look over his face and tears began to roll down his face, and it just hurt all of our hearts. Again, we'd had another tearful moment where we all had to draw from each other's strength out of pain over losing Tarrence. Just when we thought it was getting better for us celebrating the holidays it often seems to stay the same.

February 15, 2008: It's a little past three years since my son has been gone, and as I ride through the neighborhood that encompasses the area and the hospital where he spent much of his time during some of the last days of his life. I instantly develop a feeling of sadness and a heavy heart as a reminder of the pain that accompanied me that very evening of November 25, 2005, as I pass the hospital.

As I think again about so many things about that evening all over, such as how I felt came rushing back, the tears begin to roll down my face uncontrollably, as I remembered that dreadful night I lost my child at that very spot.

I think to myself this neighborhood is such a painful reminder of my loss and the pain that I now endure, each time I come face to face with certain memories or reminders of how he was murdered, in a neighborhood called K-Town "The Square."

I visit the cemetery fairly often; it gives me a sense of calm, and strength in a strange way and closeness when I feel I need it. Tarrence Jr. may sometimes accompany me, when we are passing the cemetery he always says "hi da da and he waves as though his dad can see him wave."

March 7, 2007: As I drive Tarrence comes to mind and these words are laid on my heart, so I decided to write them below and dedicate them to my son this poem is to my son.

I Miss You
By Denice Hayes

I Miss you so my Dear Son
I miss seeing your face with that beautiful warm smile
that seemed to brighten the day and light up the room.

I miss hearing your voice and that certain way you
called me Ma
I miss that tender embrace, and the mother/son kiss
we shared.
And as I look around you seem to be hidden in so
many places
I miss you so,
There are so many memories of you all around.
Memories in that young man who dresses like you
once did.
That special walk, where you took your time, never
getting in a hurry
Memories when I hear your favorite song on the radio
or a song that reminds me of you
Memories when the telephone rings, and I remember
when I was able to hear your voice on the other end,
or wish I could.
The memories still exist in certain parts of the house
Memories of seeing your car parked in front of the
house at your grandma's and when you would visit
me and pull up in the drive right at the door.
Memories of you when I drive through the area you
once hung out, and the hurt and sadness it brings
when it reminds me that it is where you once hung
out, and now only memories dwell.
And then I remember the sadness and pain that I've

had to endure because you are no longer with me,
only the memories of what used to be your existence
now dwells.
I love and Miss you more than words could ever
express.

~ You will forever be in my heart... ~ Love Mom

These words express exactly the feelings I get when I am driving through the old neighborhood or areas that Tarrence has history in or hung around and even in passing the Hospital on the West Side of Chicago where he died, or the square where he was shot:

Empty Places

From the book:
"Stars in the Deepest Night – After the Death of a Child"
Author: Genesse Bourdeau Gentry

I drove the old way yesterday, it's been a while you see.

And there, without warning, the pain washed over me.

I drove the old way yesterday and sadness came on so strong!

I was taken back, by so many feelings, since you've been gone.

Places seem to lie and wait to summon up the tears, to say remember Yesterday.

Those days when you were here, places you once laughed

And played, these are the places I now cry. These places hold memories

That will live as long as I.

March 18, 2008: Thank God with time Tarrence's loss has gotten more controllable, there are many times still that I think of him or a certain situation that draws tears, and the pain still seems as fresh as it did on that evening of November 25th, and I have come to the conclusion that the pain may never go away because in many ways that is the same as a scar received from a fall or bad relationship, it embeds into the heart forever.

As this month approached even before the thought of his birthday has been in the back of my mind, no matter when it comes I think of how excited he got about his birthday because to him it was a holiday. In a way it was his own holiday, and he had to do something special to celebrate it.

This year he would be 31 years old and we plan to as always visit his final resting place on that day, release balloons as a sign to him of our love and remembrance on his special day. My mom celebrates her birthday the following day so we also go to dinner or something in honor of them both.

(Reflection) I remember when Tarrence was born March 28, 1977 at 4:11p.m. in Chicago, Illinois. I had an eleven hour labor with him and he was born crying. I thought that moment was one of the greatest ever to experience in my life, to give birth to another life. Losing him to murder was definitely the worst experience to ever endure.

My mom said that since Tarrence was born on the 28th of March and her birthday followed on the 29th he was her birthday gift, her first grandchild.

We often talked about Tarrence and how he was what many call a free spirit. He loved outdoors, music, clothes, and women of course. He enjoyed movies but action movies were his favorite, and most of all he was spontaneous, he did things at the spur of the moment with little or no planning, I think he liked the adventure that came with it. I often teased my mom saying that she and Tarrence reflected the March weather in their actions because they tend to be so unpredictable.

It makes me sad to remember the way Tarrence died because he was such a loving and warm-hearted, compassionate person. It seems so hard to imagine that someone could dislike him enough to kill him, or even dislike him. He was a delightful and very respectful young man. Yes he had some infractions with the law but he had never done any time.

I found a thank you letter from the Secretary of State relating to him having signed up to become an Organ Donor in the event that something happen to him. And when I saw the letter it brought sadness and tears because I said to myself here is yet another example of selfless Tarrence was and the goodness that exists in his heart, yet someone has taken his life.

And at that moment I decided to honor his wish to be an Organ Donor. So when the Gift of Hope came to us once it had been determined that he would not get better, and was brain dead, with the thought of him being a Donor I agreed.

At first I was not sure I had done the right thing, many things went through my mine. Then one day in January

2006, in the mail was an envelope from the Gift of Hope addressed to me. I paused and thought to myself, why they are writing me? So I anxiously and nervously opened the envelope to find a letter that read, enclosed is a sealed letter from one of the recipients of Tarrence's Organ Donation. I stood there for a moment emotions began to raise and bounce around, with anxiety for some reason the nervous thought of what I might read I guess.

I finally opened the letter and oh my God I cried so after reading the letter, all I could do was sit down, this person talked about how grateful he and his family were for the gift of another opportunity that Tarrence had given him, knowing that in order for him to donate his organ I had suffered a tremendous loss myself. And at that moment I knew that the gift of Organ Donation for Tarrence had been the right thing to do. I felt such a sense of gratification and the thought Wow! Tarrence is living on and he has made an important difference in this person's life.

His Organ Donation gave me the sense that a part of him is still alive and living that adventure that he loved so much and it gave me a sense of peace with his being gone, because in an unusually scientific way he still lives on, he lives on in others and that makes my heart very happy to know that in his death he still touched lives in a positive way by giving a part of himself.

And I am happy to say that what "The devil meant his death for evil, but God has turned it to good" because five people today have the opportunity to live a better quality of life because "my child" at twenty eight he made the most selfless decision a person can make, which was to donate his organs and this selfless act Blessed five individuals. I am also happy to say that I have had written contact with five of six of his Recipients, and contact with one at their request on a fairly regular basis.. "**Thank you God,**" I can finally see signs of the joy that cometh in the morning.

I had joined a Ministry at my Church, its mission started out to serve, as a ministry that would reach out to those who had lost loved ones, which is what drew my interest in it. It ended up being ironic that I would end up being one to have to be on the other side of the ministry not long after joining it.

I stayed with the ministry and the following year I had the opportunity of assisting with planning this annual dinner, which the ministry sponsored for those who had lost loved ones. I also had been given the task of choosing a scripture from the Bible to read at the dinner and this is what I chose.

One thing I do, forgetting those things, which are behind and reaching forward to those things which are ahead, I press toward the goal for the prize of the upward call of God in Christ Jesus.

Philippians 3:13-14

Parental Grief
Parental grief is boundless. It touches every aspect of [a] parent's being... parents grieve for the rest of their lives.

Their grief becomes part of them... that grief is [their] link to the child. [Their] grief keeps [them] connected to the child. Arnold and Gemma, 1996

Bereaved parents continue to be parents of the child who died. They will always, feel the empty place in their hearts caused by the child's death; (Wisconsin Perspectives Newsletter – Spring 1989

March 28, 2008: Today my Son, if living would turn thirty-one years old. All this week he has especially been heavy on my mind and heart, thinking about his Birthday and how we will celebrate without him. As I lay in bed and midnight rolled around I whispered in a low voice Happy 31st Birthday baby. I had done well emotionally all day but as we drove to the cemetery, my mine began to wander and the tears began to fall, thinking how I wish that it had not had to come to this. Thinking about yet another Birthday in which I had to acknowledge his birthday in the cemetery because of some heartless person.

As we arrived I could not help but have a heavier heart and sadness because there was another family still there in his section saying goodbye to their loved one and I could not help but think of the pain that I imagine that they must be experiencing at that moment, and I watched as a young man stood being consoled by another as he struggled to compose himself before he could get into his car to depart the cemetery.

And yet again the tears began to fall in sadness as I thought to myself, I to could relate all so well whether I wanted to or not, I felt the sadness, the hurt, the pain that this person must be feeling because I too felt it in the loss and absence of my only child who also lay in this cold, lonely place where he now occupies undesired space, where we took flowers, released

balloons and spent limited time talking with him for the third year, all the while wishing we were there for any other reason but to visit him there.

April 11, 2008: Tarrence had experienced several instances where he had been hurt because he hung around the wrong crowd, I guess being an only child he had that desire to belong or fit in, a desire to have friends. I remember one evening we got a call that he was in the emergency room with a head injury. My sister, two nieces my husband and I rushed to the emergency room at Bethany Hospital on the West Side. Tarrence had a bad habit of thinking he could trust people he shouldn't, he always wanted to believe everyone had good in them and he could be friends with them. Not realizing in this age you can hardly trust anyone.

Tarrence was there and we were told that he was dropping someone off somewhere on the West Side of Chicago. He saw someone he knew began to talk to them outside the car and someone else came up behind him and hit him in the head with something that knocked him unconscious. He had a knot the size of a golf ball on his head.

They took his leather jacket, jewelry, cell phone and his wallet and left him lying on the ground next to his car in the winter with no coat. A girl who knew him saw his car. She saw him laying there and took him to the emergency room. She knew Tarrence's girlfriend, so she sent someone to her house to let her know what had happened, and his girlfriend called us. He was so hurt after dialing his cell phone, because he recognized the voice of the person who answered his cell phone. They were the ones who had robbed him of earlier.

Another time he and a couple friends were in a restaurant on the west side a little past midnight eating. Some Spanish guys came in, words were exchanged and my son said that one guy tried to punk him and as he was talking to one guy another, hit him in the face with a bottle and then pulled a gun on them and robbed them of their money and jewelry. The restaurant staff did nothing.

These were a couple of the instances that Tarrence encountered as he traveled the streets of the west side of Chicago. And he was the kind that wanted to be that strong man and I was afraid for him out in the streets and always had a fear of a late night phone call that turned out to be at 5 in the evening, nothing like I thought it would be. He was shot literally in the daytime. These instances still didn't seem to deter him from the tough areas in which he traveled and so I would just be so afraid for him.

One Saturday morning as I lay in the bed praying I said Lord, here is your child I give him to you to look after and gave Tarrence back to God, I remember saying to God that if I had a choice I would rather see Tarrence in jail than dead because at least I would be able to see his face, hear his voice and I know this was selfish because he would have probably wanted it the other way around since he was an outdoors person, confinement would have killed the free spirit he had.

Tarrence was a very restless spirited person, and not that he was bad, into trouble or anything, he just was one of those young people that liked to wander all through the night. Tarrence didn't have a sense of time when it came to coming home. I would always tell him that the early hours were the times for trouble, and that was always my fear.

As I prayed I said to God, I know I pray so often to you about my child, asking your protection of him, and I was so tired of worrying, and being afraid for him in the streets, I was unable to sleep knowing he may be out late somewhere; or was in fear when the telephone would ring after midnight, thinking it's a call about him because he had several issues with so called friends that he trusted that had betrayed him in one way or another. Some owed him money and never paid it back, with others it was jealousy he would tell me.

I know that God loved him every bit as much as I did. I couldn't begin to think what kind of suffering God had experienced, when he lost his only child to Sinners that were strangers and knowing the way Jesus was crucified, even though he rose again. And at that moment I said to God here is your child I turn him back to you, you gave him to me on loan, let your will be done only you know what's best for him even better than I. About few months later Tarrence would be shot and killed.

I sometimes wonder to myself if his death was a result

of my prayer to God that morning? Was that what it meant, giving him back to God? As I think about it, in many ways it was, he's gone off this earth. It wasn't what I meant when I gave him back to God but is that what God felt, I guess was actually best? I have always believed that God knows best, and whatever happens there is a reason for it. Since praying that morning, I have had a nagging thought and question if that prayer played any role in my son's death, sometimes regretting the prayer, and wondering if it might have made a difference in him still being here or not?

My Aunt has always told to be careful what you pray for because you have power in the tongue to speak life or death, and you should know what you pray for as well, because God may give you what you ask for and you may not want it when he gives it to you. This too was in the back of my mine.

I told my husband one day it seemed so strange, remembering how often I prayed for my son, asking God to keep him and protect him, and now that he is gone, it seems so weird to not be doing it because it had been such a routine to pray for him constantly, and now he's dead.

chapter eight
thank god for carrying us

There is no tragedy like the death of a child, things never get back to the way they were.
"Dwight D. Eisenhower"

The thing about losing my son is that I have experienced so many different feelings. I remember I couldn't sleep I would walk the floor until the early hours of the morning. My brain wouldn't shut off; I was constantly thinking about so many things. I did so much crying in private. And I had so many questions and no answers.

All I could see was my son and in my mind thousands of times the many different scenarios that I was told had happened, and what might have happened. All I knew was that each time I thought about how he might have died, it felt as though my heart was being ripped out again, I was angry, hurt and sad. I felt that he was unjustly killed and was getting no justice for his death.

As I sit here typing I re-live that day once more and the tears roll down my face as I remember the hurt and pain again. It's now two years and five months later and no one in custody, and no calls from the police at all relating to the case. There are so many things our bodies go through when we lose loved ones; especially our children and although it's a guaranteed part of living, it is not something I wish even on my worst enemy.

If the loss of a child doesn't make you strong it will most certainly break you if you allow it to, that's why it is so important for any of us that experience the death of a loved one not only a child, to seek counseling or a support group as a means of dealing with and getting through the grief. Even the toughest person dealing with the death of a loved one will go through traumatic changes while attempting to cope with the grief associated with the loss.

There are many moods, feelings, emotions that are associated with death.

April 25, 2008: In spite of the rain, lighting and wind today we celebrated my sister's birthday. The harder we try to move forward with our lives individually (though never forgetting) when we all come together even when that loved one is not there, they actually are.

I sit here with tears in my eyes and a sad heart today because no matter what, Tarrence is always brought into our gathering when we get together. I guess no matter how things change, they stay the same and he is always on our hearts and minds and in our spirits. And he is always a part of the many good times we've shared as a family.

My life isn't the same since that dreaded day after Thanksgiving Day, November 25, 2005, the day that turned our lives upside down and took us into a tailspin. It seems as if our lives are on pause, waiting for something that we know will never happen, and as much as it is a reality, it still somehow seems to still be somewhat of a dream.

I guess the more I think about what others say that have lost mothers, fathers, and loved ones is that you don't get over it but you learn to get through it. Some have said after many years, the pain never goes away that you will always miss that loved one.

The more I think about my situation and wonder how long will it be for me before I am at a point where I can actually say I'm truly better wholeheartedly? I wonder sometimes if there is such a time. If I will ever totally come close to a point of closure that will bring me a peace that will release the hurt and pain that still inhibits my body and soul?

As I go on with life as best I can, I hold on to that old saying that Joy will come in the morning, so I had to take a moment to evaluate where my heart is at this point? At what level am I in the grieving process today after almost three years, compared to when my son's murder first happened? Where is my level on pain? Am

I stuck still trying to accept the reality of it all? Has it gotten better at all?

Should I seek psychological help to find myself in all the grief of losing my child?

As I write this book I evaluate myself on this scale I believe that I am between 6-9 on the pain scale, because though I have moved on with my life I still have occasional sadness and tears, but I am able to talk about him now and smile, while sometimes his memories still brings sadness and tears. I believe that I will always miss him and that void will forever remain. I am able to say that I am now able to control my grief and getting through it.

May 11, 2008: Today is Mother's Day and this marks near the third year of my son's murder. And **I thank God** because it has actually been better than I imagined. Yes there have been tears and some sadness, but I have stood on God's word saying that he would never leave me and I know that it was during my time of grief that he truly carried me and yes, I now see light at the end of the tunnel.

Take a moment to evaluate yourself, see where you are on the Pain Scale to see if you are on the road to healing yet? Or are you standing still? Go ahead take the challenge on the below.

GRIEF/PAIN SCALE

Grieving Severely	Grief is better	grief controllable	No change
100%	75%	50%	25%

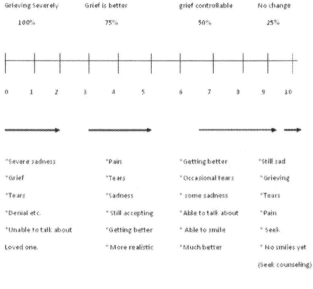

| 0 | 1 | 2 | 3 | 4 | 5 | 6 | 7 | 8 | 9 | 10 |

*Severe sadness	*Pain	*Getting better	*Still sad
*Grief	*Tears	*Occasional tears	*Grieving
*Tears	*Sadness	*some sadness	*Tears
*Denial etc.	*Still accepting	*Able to talk about	*Pain
*Unable to talk about	*Getting better	*Able to smile	*Seek
Loved one.	*More realistic	*Much better	*No smiles yet
			(Seek counseling)

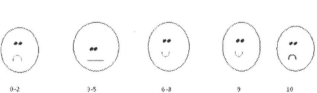

| 0-2 | 3-5 | 6-8 | 9 | 10 |

76

chapter nine
the stages of grieving

ven though we are all different, grieving can sometimes follow a loose pattern. You will go through you grief in your own unique way, but it may be reassuring to know that others may follow similar journeys. If this does not describe your journey, that is fine. There is no right way to grieve.

Author Debra Moore states that a death is like a wound. We take for granted that physical wounds require time as well as attention to heal properly. Emotional wounds are the same, though we often neglect to give them either the time or attention they deserve. When this happens, we may get stuck in our grief, and our sadness may turn to depression or simmering anger. You may be surprised to hear that psychologists do not expect the grieving process to be completed for about two years if the death is of a spouse or child. If the grieving process is allowed to run its natural course, this is a pattern you may experience.

Stage I: Breaking Old Habits
(Time of death to about eight weeks)

Immediately after a death, feelings of numbness, acute pain, anger, or powerlessness may overcome you. Many decisions need to be made at this time and they may seem overwhelming. Countless routine habits remind you of your loved one and of your loss. You probably feel deep sadness and loneliness. During this period a grieving person may experience changes in appetite and sleeping habits. These disturbances generally last only a short time and clear up eventually. If they do not, this may be a sign that you may want to seek professional counseling to talk about your feelings.

You may also decide to seek counseling if you are having a difficult time allowing your feelings to emerge. Unexpected tears now are normal and help you move through your grief. Holding them back is not helpful and may actually prolong your grief. Being preoccupied with your loved one is also normal during this first stage. Many people report a sense of the deceased one's presence, and psychologists do not regard these experiences as abnormal at all. In fact, continuing to "talk" to your loved one may provide comfort at this time. This first stage is not the time to make important life changes. It is a time to be as kind to yourself as possible.

Stage II: Beginning to Reconstruct Your Life
(Eight weeks to one year)

You will probably continue to experience emotional unsettledness during this first year. You may be more prone to illness or accidents, may continue to have bouts of sleep disturbance or change in appetite, and may begin to cry unexpectedly, perhaps when seeing a scene on television that reminds you of a time with your loved one. You may experience lapses of memory or carelessness.

Some survivors may now attempt to self-medicate with alcohol or other drugs. If you begin to depend on these substances, take an honest look at yourself and get professional help now. Things are likely to get worse without it. You may find yourself thinking of suicide. If these thoughts linger or if they frighten you, seek out professional help to talk about them. A counselor will not think you are crazy because you have had suicidal thoughts, but will help you be sure you never act on them. During this first year, holidays and special dates are particularly painful. Remember that each year it will get easier. This is not the way it is always going to feel. By the anniversary of the death, you will be aware of some changes in yourself. You have a way to go, but can begin to look towards the future.

Stage III: Seeking New Love Objects or Friends (One year to two years)

If you have been allowing yourself to grieve, you will probably now notice that many routines have returned to normal. You may be sleeping, eating, remembering, and concentrating better. You can laugh again and seldom cry unexpectedly. You continue to think of the deceased, but not as often or with as much intensity. You are not as prone to illness or accidents. You have probably made some new friends by now, and have shared your experiences with them. You have probably started planning leisure activities more often, and are less lonely and more involved. If you are working, you are able to be as productive as before the death of your loved one. Your thinking is sharper and more focused.

If this does not describe you at this point in your grieving, please consider talking to someone. If you are totally uncomfortable with the idea of seeing a professional counselor, you should at least open up to a close friend or family member, and you should also consider seeking professional help, to guide you through this traumatic time in your life and remember that you can go for only one visit or as many as you need.

**Stage IV: Readjustment completed
(After the second year)**

At this final stage, you have settled into your new life and activities. Things feel normal and routine. At times you feel quite content. You can look easily toward the future. Knowing that you have survived this loss tells you that you can survive anything. You know that pain eases in time and the wounds in your heart have healed. You may feel like a different person - and you are. You have changed and grown. If you have allowed the pain of your grief to be experienced, you have been rewarded with renewed hope and courage.

Stages of Grieving:
Denial: shock and disbelief.

Bodily Distress: anxiety can cause physical or emotional

symptoms such as loss of appetite, obsessive eating, exhaustion, sleeplessness, and nightmares.

Anger: outward expressions of hostility, rage, explosive behavior or inward expressions of depression, self-blame or self-destructive ideation.

Hostile Reactions to the Deceased: feelings of being deserted, abandoned or rejected.

Hostile Reactions to Others: blaming others such as mother/father, God, doctor.

Guilt/Self-Blame: "If only I hadn't done____", guilt over comments such as "I wish you were dead" or "I hate you".

Bargaining: buying time to accept the reality of the situation.

Replacement: a child quickly seeks affection from others as a substitute.

Assumptions of Mannerisms: the child takes on characteristics of the loved one.

Tries to carry out the plans or wishes of the one that died.

Idealization: the child is obsessed with positive qualities.

Depression: feelings of helplessness, hopelessness, withdrawal, loss of pleasure.

Anxiety: preoccupation with physical symptoms. School avoidance is common.

Panic: state of confusion and shock. A period of fearfulness exists regarding others.

Acceptance: Child learns to reorganize his/her life without the dead loved one.

May 26, 2008: Memorial Day, but also the day that my Tarrence was pronounced dead in November 2005, so I went to spend time at the cemetery I took two new flowers, but as I turned in I was in awe seeing the many people that were there, visiting their loved ones. As I drove to the section where my son was laid to rest, I looked around at the many people in the many sections of the cemetery a thought came to my mind. I thought to myself, we carry a child nine months, give birth to that child and the natural instinct is a lifelong unconditional love for that child for the rest of their live and yours.

And I thought to myself a Mother's love, this is a love so deep, so strong, immeasurable and we never stop to think how deep that love reaches, because as parents we naturally love our children with all our hearts (or should), a mother is generally a nurturer, we never stop to truly mentally measure the depth of that love nor how deep down inside it truly touches until faced with dealing with the unbearable pain of that child's death/murder, you then are forced to think about how to the core that pain reaches, and the unbearable grief that seems to reach deeper than can be expressed.

The pain feels as though it reaches down into your soul, a place that you have never visited before and didn't know existed until that moment. This very excruciating pain is a pain experienced or understood only upon the loss of a child it is an experience that has a trickledown effect. It not only touches immediate family, but extended family, friends, teachers, neighbors, co-workers, and even others in many odd ways.

May 30, 2008: As I sat at the kitchen table staring out of the window, I thought about something I used to hear "Until you walk a mile in my shoes", as I thought about my life over the past two and half years, I know that only a person that has walked in my shoes." can begin to understand what it is like to lose a child, then to lose an only child to something as tragic as murder, and the grieving process that accompanies it.

Many people don't understand why some may grieve longer than others they have known or why a person may be still shedding tears two years later at the mention of that person's name, or some may be still be holding onto clothing items of their deceased child, or others may not be able to see pictures or talk about it at all, and another person may be able to.

The grieving process is one that cannot be explained, it's a process that affects each individual differently and each individual grieves or deals with it in a different way. As well as with the length of time it takes some to get to the point where it is controllable in their life and not in control of their life. There are those who have totally shut down at the loss of their child, they could not accept it mentally. There are those who may need or have needed counseling to get them through the tougher times or to a point where they could take control of their lives again.

One thing I say about this process is that it's the most devastating emotional time in a person's life, to lose a child and until you lose one you can never know what we go through, you can only imagine.

June 1, 2008: In a few days my grandson will be nine years old and every day I think about how he must miss his dad and how is he dealing with this loss mentally, because I know how hard it has been for me daily. Also on special days like his dads birthday I know he thinks about the fact that his dad isn't here. Once when he was playing basketball and they were asking some of the other dads to volunteer as coaches, he said to me Grandma I wish my da da was here so he could be a coach, and this is such a sad reality check for us that he is gone, a confirmation of our loss that always taps us on the shoulder or slaps us in the face, reminding us that he's gone and not coming back.

I try to do special things, answer questions but you can only do so much, some things just will never take the place of spending time with your dad or that gift from your dad or that birthday call, it has a different place and meaning in itself. And I understand that because I love my grandson with every breath, and I am thankful to God for him, and as much as he is like his dads twin, it in no way substitutes the absence of his dad. My heart still longs for another glance, a whisper of his voice, or another embrace, the void remains, the sadness still resides, and the memories still are followed with tears. Yet I press on because I must and I know that he would not want it any other way.

One thing he used to always tell me was not to worry about him; and, I would tell him wait until you have kids, because that's easy to say, and so hard to do. I remember something my mom would say that her mom used to tell her also which I didn't understand at that time, it was when your children are young they are on your lap, and when they grow up they are on your heart. I now know all too well what that saying means, and now my heart carries the weight of my son lost to murder.

June 4, 2008: I think about my grandson and how well he is doing in school, it makes me sad that my grandson had to endure such hurt and pain at such a young age. It makes me even sadder when I imagine how he hurts, and the sadness he must feel inside.

Something we as adults sometimes lose sight of is what the kids must be going through also, because they grieve too, and how hard it must be for them as children to sort through all of the pain themselves, not knowing how.

One night as my grandson and I shared some time talking he said to me, "Grandma I want to stay the age I am, I don't want to get older because if I get older I might forget how my da da's voice sounded and when he used to call me boo boo and at my age now I still remember." He then said, my mom has nothing of my da da's to remember him except pictures, she doesn't have t-shirts or anything like that."

And I said to him, baby your mom has something even better and more important than anyone else, she has you, and when we look at you we see your dad in you" and he said uh! As if thinking in his mind, I never thought of it that way, he then hugged me, as to say that I had given him comfort in what I had shared with him, and he was okay with it.

That moment touched my heart in a way that made it such a sad moment that I had to struggle to hold back the tears, because to me that was a sign of his pain and his struggles to remember his dad.

June 15, 2008: Father's Day and we'd just returned from Disney World. As I lay in bed thinking about my son on today, still finding it weird that he is no longer with us, I whispered a Father's Day wish to him, and as I lay there thinking I heard Tarrence Jr. wake up. He didn't come into the bedroom but I heard him say in his little voice "Happy Father's Day Da da." After a while he came into my room, Grandma it's Father's Day, did you forget to wish my da da a Happy Father's Day? And I said no, I had already done so and that I said to him I plan to visit the cemetery today as well, and he smiled.

August 9, 2008: And it is the day after the wedding of my niece who had a relationship with Tarrence that was more of sister/brother than cousins because they grew up together. And she did something that I thought was so special.

She included two photographs of Tarrence at the Wedding Banquet hall, One 5x7 on the reserved family table and another on the table up front where she stood to take her vows. She said Aunty I know he would be here if he could so I brought his picture so that he would share tonight with us. I thought that was so special that I had to fight back the tears. Since his murder, no matter how happy the occasion, when the family gets together it is a reminder to me the reality of his death. I know that he will always be with the family.

As hard as I have tried to move on with my life there still lies a secret place in my heart where I still mourn with sadness and it has been two years, nine months sixteen days since Tarrence was murdered this date but somehow no matter how the days add up, the pain still hurts as though it was yesterday.

"Our lives rest in the hands of the One who knows all of the what's, why's, and when's we'll ever face. As we trust him, he'll guide us in the path He desires us to take – His way is never wrong, although it may not always be what we would do and may often be hard for us to accept."

Since the death of my son Tarrence I began to collect articles of murders and pay more attention to the murders of young people especially of young men, and it seems to be a never- ending tragedy for some mother or father.

I wish that there was something that I could do to make it stop, all I do is think about the pain this other person is having to endure at the hand of someone else, senselessly and that's what hurts more, that your child has lost his life over something meaningless.

I found overwhelming murder stats below, that I would like to share in hopes that on paper, in black and white those committing the killings can see the impact on these families and the tremendous numbers that they have caused by murdering senselessly and will "**STOP THE VIOLENCE!"**

The Murder Research Statistic collected from the FBI. GOV Offense data show that:

White Male murders average 5,205 White, Black 6,042, and other races 286 and 150 unknown races. With an estimated 1,390,695 violent crimes occurred nationwide in 2005. Statistics also State that there is evidence that points strongly to a 5.5 greater likelihood of young black people falling victim to violent and weapon-enabled crime, including homicide.

GUNS AND HOMICIDE

FBI Data also showed that in:

2005: 75% of murders involved a firearm and 11% were the result of a stabbing. 41% of domestic murders were stabbings. 10% of murders in 2005 (39) were the result of an armed robbery, 9% were of undetermined cause, and at least 30% were gang altercations. Over 40% of victims and 60% of offenders were between the ages of 17 and 25.

Murder is like a violent thief in the night, causing great suffering. Death leaves behind human pain and suffering, the funerals of murder victims often attract large crowds, but once the ceremonies are over, few remain with the bereaved to help dry their tears or relieve the burden of their pain. Family members are encouraged to recover and heal from the violent wound in their emotional fabric, but no one tells them how to heal.

chapter ten
recognizing our loss

On November 25, 2008: I began cooking food for the holiday and as I stir around in the kitchen cooking spaghetti, with the aroma of greens cooking on the back of the stove I think about how Tarrence would call to see what we were cooking for the holidays and asking about certain foods, such as spaghetti and greens and then asking to add peppers because he enjoyed a touch of hot pepper in his greens. As I cook the memory of his requests for his favorites things that I cooked made me think of what he would be missing, it made me sad, then the tears came from nowhere, rolling down my face like an automatic button was there or something, I can hardly see what I am doing because the tears blur my vision.

Holidays have long stopped being a highlight for me since Tarrence was killed; it seems that I don't have that same joy anymore that I once had. I still enjoy seeing my family but I guess holidays will never be the same. When we get together and Tarrence is nowhere to be found this is still a rather painful reality for me.

As the time approaches the painful memories remind me of that horrible phone call my mind begins to go into rewind and the memories of that evening, on the day after Thanksgiving when we had to take that long anxious ride to the hospital to face a tragic reality that would crush the world we that know.

On November 26, 2008: As I stood in my kitchen two minutes before the time that it was officially announced that there was nothing more they could do for him as he was pronounced brain dead at 11:58 a.m. I will never forget it, and three years later I still can't believe that Tarrence is actually gone, it still seems as though it's not real, but as the sadness creeps in we are reminded that it's no nightmare but a reality that someone has murdered my son.

As I cooked and Tarrence Jr. sat in the kitchen at the table out of nowhere he says to me well grandma I guess we will have another terrible Thanksgiving, and I say to him what do you mean? trying to avoid the obvious, he says to me because my da da won't be celebrating with us again, and I said yes that's true but we will have to think of him and his memory of how he loved the holidays, and hope that his spirit is celebrating with us, be thankful for our other family members and enjoy them.

November 27, 2008: Thanksgiving Day For the first time since Tarrence was murdered my family actually spent the holiday at home, not visiting and no company because this year especially has been an exceptionally hard year for us all and we had no momentum and that usual holiday spirit was buried a bit deeper this year than in the past and so we cooked but spent the day reminiscing in our own way about what was, is and had been.

March 28, 2009: Tarrence would have made 32 years old this day, and for the first time since his murder I didn't go to the cemetery to spend time with him on his special day because I was spending time with family out of town for the first time in many years. I did however go to the cemetery on March 26th leaving flowers and a birthday balloon, but I have thought about him for some time prior to his birthday, it seems that certain times he is heavier on my mind or in my spirit than others and the month prior to his birthday was one of those times.

May 10, 2009: Today is the fourth Mother's Day without my son. However this year I did not attend the cemetery on Mother's day but spent the day with family. It was also the second birthday of the youngest grandson in the family.

I had the opportunity to talk at great length to my Daughter in laws mom who had lost her daughter to murder five months after I lost Tarrence, although her murderer of her child was apprehended, as the conversation progressed, the hurt, pain, anguish, and the many levels of grief appeared, and the feelings of emotions and the tears drew us near, but we both held back. At that moment I again thought to myself that it's been almost four years, since I lost my son and it seems that no matter how long I go when those emotions are summoned, it all seems so fresh and brand new again. This was a revelation that I may never be the same again emotionally after this tragic separation of my son from this earth and me.

May 30, 2009: Memorial Day, My husband, Tarrence Jr. and I went to the cemetery to visit Tarrence on the holiday. We stayed a while, cleaned up around his headstone, took pictures, we planted a flowering bush above his headstone and then we had to leave him.

June 8, 2009: Tarrence Jr. just turned 10 years old and also got out of school for the summer. He made the honor role for the fourth year. Going through much of the school work from the year that has just ended I found something that really helped me to know that he is still carrying his dad in his heart even though he was young when it happened 6 yrs old. I found the item below in a project book from one of his classes at school and it was so touching I thought I would include it as a last expression of how he has held on to and dealt with in his own way the pain and anguish of losing his dad.

Sketch by Tarrence Jr. of Day my family changed

Blessed are the poor in spirit, for theirs is the
Kingdom of heaven. Blessed are those who mourn;
for they shall be comforted.
Matthew 5: 3-4

December 4, 2008: God works in mysterious ways!
I met Marilyn White, a lady I once prayed for, because
she too had been a victim of Societies crime, losing
her daughter Danielle White to a violent crime years
earlier, Mrs. White's daughter was a class mate and
friend of my son Tarrence in grade school. I remember
taking Tarrence and my niece to Danielle's funeral.
Mrs. White had come to the support group as a guest
of the Founder Phyllis Duncan; unknowingly we also
attended the same Church.

I found a picture that had been taken years prior which
I shared with Marilyn White of Tarrence and Danielle,
a Graduation picture from their eighth Graduation.

Danielle's murderer would finally be captured years

late. This mom and I thought how ironic that our paths crossing years later, and our children who were once friends would both be murdered at different times in life, though my son's murder is still unsolved. We agreed that it had to be God that led us to meet years later. My son and Danielle were very good friend in school, he wore a tattoo on his chest in her memory.

From the day I received the call about Tarrence and all that has gone on that day, has been replayed in my mind a thousand times from the beginning when it first happened, but during the time he was killed painfully replays itself on and around those dates like clockwork each year.

And as the emotions and thoughts were so caught up in that it was that time of year again somehow today I realized for the first time since his murder that the date he was buried had past me. I then thought to myself is this yet another sign that a mental healing is taking place or was the reason the date slipped by me was because I in the back of my mind didn't want to remember this day that signified a final goodbye to my only child.

Nonetheless another year begins itself and I continue to take each day, one day at a time, some days more than others remembering and fighting with the pain of those memories of my loss. When I support other women who are going through what I have, it re-opens wounds that I am trying to allow to heal. Again these painful memories are resurrected as you try to help other women to deal with the pain and tragedy of their loss.

And as you remember how painful it is because you have experienced it you can't say to them don't cry, because they have experienced a great loss in losing their child and have the right to cry and grieve, to be broken hearted, angry and many other feelings that encompass our bodies as we deal with this monster they call grief.

All I can say is that it does get easier to deal with as time passes. I don't believe the pain of losing a child ever leaves. There's a void where the love for that child once lived, it takes their place. I say to each person who loses or has lost a child, to hold on to Jesus for strength and peace because it is not an easy road to travel by far.

It's a long, dark, cold, painful road to walk and only strength will enable you to walk that painful road, and the peace of God will help you deal with it mentally. So, to all you mothers who have walked that road called grief, I say to you look to the hills from whence cometh your health and strength.

I hope that this interpretation of the grief, suffering and pain that I endured after the loss of my son will be a source of help and understanding for those who may go through it, and that it will be a source of reference in understanding all that you may endure mentally and physically when you lose a child especially to a crime as violent as murder. I truly believe that heightens the grief that you will now endure, making it a tougher battle to fight.

I also want to serve as reference that it won't be easy

but that you too can get through it with lots of prayers, support, strength, family and counseling.

And as I close wishing you God's peace and strength allow me to share a special poem with you.

Those who don't know how to weep with their whole heart don't know how to laugh either.

When we lose a loved one to death or end a long-term relationship, it is perfectly normal to grieve. We must understand and except, there is no death; there is no end' there is only transformation. Our loved one now exist in a new time, a new place, a new reality –

I will take the time to grieve and prepare myself for the change.

By: Iyanla Vanzant

GRIEF SUPPORT RESOURCES:

MOMS – Mothers of Murdered Sons
429 South 24th Avenue
Bellwood, IL 60104
Meetings: Bellwood Library
600 Bohland Avenue
Bellwood, IL 60104
2nd Saturday monthly
1-3pm
Contact - Phyllis Duncan, CEO/Founder
708-540-4392

Westside Chicago Chapter
POMC – Parents of Murdered Children
Mount Sinai Hospital
California Avenue at 15th Street
Chicago, Il 60608
3rd Tuesday monthly
6:30-8:30pm
Contact – Samantha Glover
773-576-8326

The Compassionate Friends
National Headquarters
PO Box 3696
Oak Brook, Il 60522
Telephone: 877-969-0010
Regional Coordinator: Mary Seibert
Telephone: 815-468-6443
Website – www.compassionatefriends.org

Homicide Support Group
Homan Square
3559 W. Arthington St.
Chicago, IL
Telephone 773-869-7217
(Call For information)

WHEN SEEKING A GRIEF COUNSELOR

Ask them about their:

- Credentials

- Training

- Theoretical Orientation

- Therapeutic Applications

- Experience in Bereavement

- Normal reactions to loss - Sadness, loneliness,

- Symptoms of Depression- Mood disorders

- You may experience Feelings of - Excessive guilt, Worthlessness,

- Physical symptoms - psychotic behavior, suicidal thoughts

- Some experience – Severe Deterioration in functions

- Denial – This can't be happening, I'll be alright

- Acceptance – I have to move on

  - ➤ There is something called the three F's for healing, that are helpful in dealing with grief:
    - o Family - 84%
    - o Friends – 74%
    - o Faith – 13%
  - ➤ There is no timeframe on grief – Bereavement is long for some than others

chapter eleven
moving forward

oday is "Mother's Day 2010" a day that I receive
with mixed feelings since my son's murder, because
even though I have carried and birthed this child into
the world, as I look around all I see are bits and pieces
as reminders that he ever existed and passed through
this life. The one true evidence is "his seed" a son who
has strong resemblance of his dad, pictures, and many
memories. The rest is just a simple paper trail.

As I sit going through documents such as Birth Certificate,
Social Security Card items which acknowledge his birth
into this world, I also find the only letter that I can ever
remember him writing, filled with personal thoughts,
promises and acknowledgements. The last document
I find is one that you hope not to see of your children
and that was his Death Certificate which confirmed the
demise of his presence twenty eight years later, and he
is gone.

His Death Certificate reads homicide, gunshot wound to the head, words that send a chilling message so strong to my brain and an emotion to my heart that I begin to cry as I read it. A life taken due to the hatred and hard heartedness of another individual for a reason not apparent to me, and meaningless them.

It's been almost five years later, yes I have found the strength to move forward with my life, "By the grace of God" I have worked since the murder; I'm eating normally, even laughing and smiling. But the truth of the matter is that as I move forward in life there's a part of me "I believe" that will never move forward, that small part of life is frozen in that sad time of life. A memory that remains as vivid as the day your world came crashing down.

Yes, I can now talk about my son and respond when he is mentioned most of the time without tears, but there are still times when I think of him or something pertaining to him and it breaks down all that strength I've acquired or thought I had. Because I still miss him to a degree that words cannot begin to express. I think of him daily and ever so much.

I sat up late one night watching the movie Lethal Weapon, Where the character Roger (A cop) first meets Martin Riggs (A transferred Cop) And everyone thinks he is psychotic or crazy, and in a segment of the movie they show him with a bullet he has put aside especially for committing suicide which he has attempted several times, putting the gun in his mouth but unable to pull the trigger. Riggs begins to look at a picture which is of him and his wife's wedding Day.

His wife who had been murdered, as he looks at the picture he begins to cry saying that every day he finds himself wanting to die because of how much he misses her and how it hurts him so bad. And as I sit watching this segment I am overwhelmed with tears, finding myself too full of the reminder of the same pain and emotion that he feels. At that moment there was a connection and understanding the depth of his grief and how if you aren't truly a strong person grief can and will take you to a place you can't imagine that you'd ever go.

Grief is truly a place that is many words, yet indescribable. And though I'd never thought of suicide, I understand how Riggs' grief could have taken him there, it taps in and takes over, it's a driving force that can and will take over if you aren't strong enough.

Tarrence's father who has been in and out of his life as a child though never too far was also very grief stricken by the sudden loss and murder of Tarrence. He was very bitter and as we were looking for many unanswered questions relating to the murder. And we have yet to get the answers we seek we have moved pass this time in hopes that one day we will get the answers we wait for. Although Tarrence's father was here in Chicago his Step-father was a strong influence in his life, and raising him after we married, Tarrence was a product of teenagers therefore his dad like many, was off living his life, though staying in touch since we had a son together. The door was always open, welcoming a relationship between them. I believed that it was and is important for children to have both parents in their lives it at all possible and for them to see adults act as such.

In Tarrence's final few years he and his dad developed a special relationship, demanding respect as we both did their relationship allowed them also to be friends. Even after the murder of our son we remain friends and stay in touch because of the grandson we share. Making every effort to remain a part of his grandson's life in hopes of playing an important role as a another male figure and role model to prayerfully help to keep Tarrence Jr. on the right path in life as well as to lavish the love of our son on the grandson. Granddad wants him to know that he is and always will be there for him, as our son knew also.

September 07, 2010: It's been almost five years since Tarrence was murdered, the phones have stopped ringing, and the small line of communication we once shared with the people sworn to serve and protect have ceased. No doubt they have put his case aside due to a lack of importance to them.

Our family has begun to move forward with our day to day lives, with a daily prayer that one day God will bring justice for Tarrence's murder. It's not an easy move forward but I do it day by day. Yes it still hurts, and there are still bad days for me but now there are more good days and memories in between that make me smile rather than cry. I still wonder sometimes if he were here what he'd be doing with himself? I wonder if he'd have more children or if he would have found that special girl by now? I no longer hear from the young lady that he dated during the time of his murder, so I can't say that she would have been the one, but I can say that prayerfully it seems as though she has moved on with her life.

So many things I will never have an answer to yet, I move forward with thanks to God above for the time we had with Tarrence, from March 28th which was twenty eight years, eight months, two days longer than someone's child lived until November 25, 2005. Of these years God blessed us by giving us a grandchild before Tarrence was taken from us and for I am so grateful. I move forward with a great deal more of appreciation for life now truly taking nothing for granted, especially another day.

As I move forward with my life I also take my role as the Administrator of MOMS Support Group very seriously, contributing my time, service also offering support to current attendees and new ones that may come to the group in need of counsel or a listening ear after having lost their child in the same manner. The passion that I have for what I do with MOMS is due to the loss of my son, whom I encouraged daily. If I can help a grieving mother, or assist in re-directing the life of a youth who has lost or is losing their way, I will reach out to them.

I think of my son and how he tried so hard to get back on track once he was side tracked losing his job, and how he felt that no one cared enough to extend a hand of trust to him, a young black man, who wanted and needed someone to care enough to give him a chance to prove himself. He was often discouraged, trying to find employment.

So, when I reach out to help especially the young men struggling to find their way, I do it in honor of my son Tarrence Darnell Parks Sr., remembering his struggles in life and trying to make a difference in the life of another young man who may be trying to better himself and find his way back to a proper place in society.

October 10, 2010: What I always say to those that I encounter who has lost a loved one whether to murder or in another form, after experiencing death/murder first hand, is to take things one day at a time, seek out counsel during your time of grief because it will play a key role in moving you through the grieving process.   As I have said grief is a pain that can't truly be described. It leaves a void that will never be filled, a hurt that stays with you and it leaves loneliness for that person that can't be met. Grief is a feeling that you learn to get through in time, however I don't believe that you ever get over the loss.

May God bless you in your quest for peace and strength in reclaiming your life after the loss of your loved one. I can say that with time the hurt and pain gets easier to deal with however, I know for certain that it is not something that you every get over it forever remains buried in your heart. Know that the clouds will clear and the sun will shine on you too again.

Surrender to God

Romans 14:4 NIV

If we live, we live to the Lord; and if we die, we die to the Lord. So, whether we live or die, we belong to the Lord.

afterword

These words are especially for the mother's
who have lost a child.
Letter to Mom
I see you are still feeling sad,
It was just my time to go
We all come to earth for our lifetime,
And for some it's not as long
By Joy Curnutt

*Mom and Grandson visiting Tarrence Sr.
at Cemetery*

reflection and farewell

Tarrence Darnell Parks Sr.
Your Memory will forever live in my heart.
Farewell my only Child, may you rest in peace.

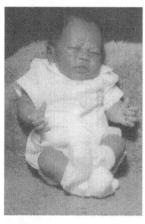

Tarrence Sr's baby picture – born March 28, 1977 at 4:11 p.m

Tarrence Sr. with Santa

Tarrence Sr.
Kindergarten Graduation

Tarrence Sr. Easter
age 14

Tarrence Sr. & Jr
spending time gaming

Tarrence Sr. 8th grade
Graduation Day

Tarrence Sr. up close
smiling

Tarrence Sr. Laying back

Tarrence Darnell Parks Sr.
Pronounced dead at 11:58 a.m.